1990

SUBSTANCE AND MODERN SCIENCE

Substance and Modern Science

RICHARD J. CONNELL

CENTER FOR THOMISTIC STUDIES ·
University of St. Thomas
3812 Montrose Boulevard
Houston, Texas 77006

Library of Congress Cataloging-in-Publication Data

Connell, Richard J.
    Substance and modern science.

    Bibliography: p.
    Inclues index.
    1. Substance (Philosophy)   2. Science—Philosophy.
I. Title.
BD311.C66   1988   111'.1   87-73319
ISBN 0-268-01731-X
ISBN 0-268-01732-8 (pbk.)

Manufactured in the United States of America

Table of Contents

PART I
The Reality of Substance

PART II
The Multiplicity of Substances

PREFACE

Lest a misunderstanding arise in the mind of the reader, let me remark at the start that the title *Substance and Modern Science* must not be taken to suggest that this is a book in the philosophy of science. Our aim here is not to consider what use current scientific theories make of the notion of substance, nor is it to investigate what the sciences might understand by the term "substance" and its applications. Instead our purpose is quite different and belongs not to the philosophy of science but to philosophy without qualification. What this means, however, needs explanation.

Richard Rorty has recently told us that Philosophy has failed in the purpose it proposed for itself when it set out to engage in systematic investigations of what we know, and that as a consequence it must come to understand that its true function is to improve human conversation. A philosopher, he thinks, is a sort of professional "needle" who must criticize society's prevailing wisdom with a view to seeing whether it all hangs together but without pretending to endorse it as definitively true,[1] and Rorty's having surrendered his chair in philosophy for one in the "humanities" shows that he acts on his convictions. Though we shall contend with Rorty about the function of philosophy, we nonetheless must admit that much of what he says is hard to deny. At the very least philosophy appears to have experienced a malaise for some time and seems to have lost confidence in what it is doing.

Since the time of Locke and Descartes philosophy has tried to confine itself to inquiries about knowledge, leaving the realm of physical, empirical reality to the natural sciences. Contemporary philosophy does not consider itself obligated to start, as do the natural and social sciences, from regularities of behavior and properties belonging to real things "out there." Philosophers have surrendered the whole of the real, physical world to the natural sciences, implicitly if not explicitly, conceding that such sciences have the last word about a domain they may rightly claim as their own. That means that philosophers who would talk about real things and their properties are, in a strong sense of the phrase, "out of bounds," even though at times people may politely listen to them. The epistemological, or its linguistic expression: that is thought to be philosophy's realm.

Historically, of course, it was not always thus. In Aristotle's time philosophy and science were one enterprise, and it was not until Newton, followed by Kant, that the divorce between the two was truly established, perhaps primarily because of the mathematical character of Newtonian physics. But whatever the reason for it, the divorce has been complete for some time; and in our day mainstream philosophy not only has no part of the real world as its domain, it also has abandoned the empirical methods and modes of explanation that characterize accounts of real things.

The point which is central to the present essay is that certain fundamental parts of philosophy must deal with physical things, and they must do so without supposing that philosophy cannot proceed without first having "established" an epistemological theory under which to do its business. In short, we wish to say that the investigation of nature cannot be left entirely to physics, chemistry, and biology; for the natural sciences cannot make sense of the world of nature all by themselves, a point that is implicitly made by Karl Popper when he says the following:

> While discussing a problem we always accept (if only temporarily) all kinds of things as *unproblematic*: they constitute for the time being, and for the discussion of this particular problem, what I call our *background knowledge*. Few parts of this background knowledge will appear to us in all contexts as absolutely unproblematic, and any particular part of it *may* be challenged at any time, especially if we suspect that its uncritical acceptance may be responsible for some of our difficulties. But almost

> all of the vast amount of background knowledge
> which we constantly use in any informal discussion
> will, for practical reasons, necessarily remain
> unquestioned; and the misguided attempt to question
> at all--that is to say, *to start from scratch*--can easily
> lead to the breakdown of a critical debate.[2]

Popper is right, of course, and few will deny that he is; for the human mind cannot enter upon a scientific enterprise of any kind with a mind completely empty of every conception derived from ordinary experience, and that is what "background knowledge" would appear to be. Popper is also right when he says that in informal discussions the background knowledge must remain unquestioned, for one cannot start from scratch in every debate; the intellectual enterprise would break down. But that leads to our point: the background knowledge presupposed to scientific investigations is itself in need of systematic investigation on the basis of the regularities ordinary experience provides, together with an appropriate logical--i.e., systematic--apparatus to direct its consideration. And that, I would contend, is the business of what we shall call "Natural Philosophy."

Although philosophy seems to have surrendered without cause its right to investigate the empirical, physical world, the philosophical problems that arise from nature do not disappear merely because philosophers are no longer in touch with them. On the contrary, the problems arise directly out of the regularities in which the sciences are immersed. One sign of this is the custom of authors who write beginning textbooks in biology and who regularly introduce their work with comments on the philosophical viewpoint which prevails in it, a viewpoint that is ordinarily chosen from two options: vitalism and mechanism. Of course vitalism is not in fashion these days, so the viewpoint adopted is ordinarily declared to be mechanistic, whether or not it is consistently maintained throughout the work. A third option sometimes offered is dialectical materialism, the official philosophical background knowledge of communist authors.

But philosophical problems also arise out of the sciences in a more sophisticated atmosphere. A recent work in cosmology, *The Anthropic Cosmological Principle*,[3] is a case in point. Chapters two and three discuss from a historical point of view some of the philosophical topics relevant to the central issue of their work.[4] So the philosophical issues will out, the reluctance of philosophers to enter the arena notwithstanding. To repeat our point, the natural sciences cannot make complete sense of the world of nature by themselves; they need the help of philosophy.

In keeping with its role of providing a systematic account of what Popper has called "background knowledge," natural philosophy bases its considerations of the physical world on ordinary, common experience; that is precisely why it provides a "background." Physical entities have certain common principles and certain common properties that can be examined without using instruments of any kind; natural philosophy examines them, and that is what makes it empirical. Its procedures are argumentative and systematic, requiring careful delineation of the data which common experience provides, unlike the sort of narrative-descriptive procedure which is found in Heidegger, say, or in Whitehead's *Process and Reality*. But unfortunately philosophers tend to feel ill at ease both with the subject matters appropriate to natural philosophy and with its empirical character. Such a feeling, however, can be overcome.

The specific problem we shall consider might be classed under several headings familiar to modern philosophers: mechanism, reductionism, or even the mind-body problem. We shall not, however, treat the issue according to the style one might expect in a contemporary journal, for every one of the above is fundamentally a problem about substance. The existence, the nature, and the multiplicity of natural substances: that might be the most general topic to indicate what we plan to study here.

As we have already indicated, we shall go about our business in an atypical fashion, one that is empirical and closely argued. And though our resolution of the philosophical problem does not depend on the data of the modern sciences, we nevertheless make considerable use of such data for reasons we have suggested above, that is, because the data provoke the scientist into reflecting on the problem. That does not mean we are addressing ourselves to biologists, chemists, and physicists. On the contrary, we are addressing ourselves primarily to philosophers in the hope that they will come to see that philosophy is properly anchored only when it is willing to face the issues as they arise naturally according to the intellectual conditions of our own time. It is true, the philosopher who deals with such topics does need some familiarity with the sciences mentioned, but he does not need an extensive exposure. Of course the more he does know about the natural sciences, the better equipped he is to illustrate the issues and to add to the inductive evidence.

Though what we have done here has been put in contemporary dress, our position is that of Aristotle, presented by him many years ago. Furthermore, we have taken advantage of one of his commentators, namely, Thomas Aquinas. But the reader ought not to expect references to the works of these authors. That we think is, in our time, counterproductive. Apart from making use of scientific data, our contemporary dress consists mainly of a more current language which eschews the vocabulary typical of the manuals of past years, on the ground that the language they use is often misunderstood. And we may add that words, after all, are not important but rather the notions and realities they manifest.

* * * * * * * * *

I would be remiss were I to close without acknowledging my indebtedness to my colleagues, especially J. M. Hubbard, who read the manuscript with considerable care and expertise, and who made many valuable suggestions. I owe thanks to Thomas Sullivan and Susan Krantz, both of the Department of Philosophy. Finally, my thanks must go to Henry B. Veatch for some helpful criticisms and suggestions that came at just the right time. Nor is it merely a matter of form when I say that the deficiencies, whatever and wherever they may be, are my own.

R. J. C.

College of St. Thomas
St. Paul, Minnesota

Notes to Preface

[1]*Philosophy and the Mirror of Nature* (Princeton University Press, 1979).

[2]*Conjectures and Refutations: The Growth of Scientific Knowledge*, Harper Torchbooks (New York: Harper & Row, Publishers, 1963), p. 238.

[3]John D. Barrow and Frank J. Tipler (New York: Oxford University Press, 1986).

[4]What has come to be called "The Anthropic Principle" is actually a very old principle, well known to Aristotle but no longer understood by philosophers. To be sure, the form in which it is stated does not correspond to the expressions of cosmologists, but the principle is the same nevertheless. We regret we cannot discuss it here.

PART I

THE REALITY OF SUBSTANCE

CHAPTER 1

THE PROBLEM

To say that natural things change is obviously true, for the proposition is verified by the commonest of observations, the kind of observations we make when our senses first begin to function. So firmly established is the proposition that we find it difficult even to conceive of some "possible world" in which change might be absent. But not only do changes occur in natural things, the various kinds of change are the center of focus for scientific investigations. Physics, we all know, investigates the movement of bodies under the influence of gravitational fields, the movements of elementary particles resulting from electromagnetic or nuclear forces, the changes that result from heating and cooling, as well as others we need not list. And though it investigates other properties, too, it does so insofar as they pertain to some kind of change.

Chemistry is another science concerned with changes, for it investigates the reactions of elements in forming compounds. Chemists, however, think that both elements and compounds are substances endowed with properties, the former distinct from the latter, as the following statement implies:

> The characteristics which enable us to distinguish
> one substance from another are known as
> properties.[1]

Moreover, chemical reactions are not, per se, modifications of
physical properties, as we see when the chemist says that

> those characteristics involved in a transformation of
> one substance into another are known as chemical
> properties.[2]

Chemical properties are not the same as physical properties, since
chemical properties are those that account for "the transformation
of one substance into another"; that is, they account for changes in
substances themselves. Although physical properties do vary as
the result of chemical reactions, a change of substance is distinct
from the change of properties that follows upon it, and that is why
physical changes can occur without there being changes that are
chemical. Hence chemistry is a science different from physics.
    When changes are looked at from the most general point of
view, therefore, those that occur in inanimate nature are
considered to be of two main kinds: *physical change* and *chemical
change.* The first is realized in the modifications of physical
properties, the second in the transformation of one substance into
another. At this point, however, we must note that when we claim
chemical reactions are either the production or the destruction of a
substance, we give rise to a problem.
    If chemical changes bring variations in substances, then there
are at least as many substances as there are different chemical
reactions; in short, the position of the chemist implies that there
are many substances in nature. But this view is not everywhere
held, for two eminent physicists implicitly contradict it when they
tell us that historically the development of physics has involved a
reduction in the number of substances required to explain natural
entities, a reduction that has continued until our own time:

> Classical physics introduced two substances: matter
> and energy. The first had weight, but the second was
> weightless. In classical physics we had two
> conservation laws: one for matter, the other for
> energy. We have already asked whether modern
> physics still holds this view of two substances and the
> two conservation laws. The answer is: "No."
> According to the theory of relativity, there is no
> essential distinction between mass and energy.[3]

According to Einstein and Infeld the two substances of classical
physics have been reduced to one in relativity physics. But if that
is so, then a chemical reaction cannot be the transformation of one
substance into another. A unitary substance as such cannot be
transformed; so if the universe is monistic, chemical reactions will
have to be understood as something other than the transformation
of one substance into another.

Before we go further let us note what biologists are inclined to
say:

> On the broadest possible level, there is the fact that
> protoplasm appears to be basically one substance,
> varied in more or less minor ways from species to
> species, throughout the living world.[4]

These lines remind us that biologists speak of protoplasm as a
"living substance," and taken at face value this is an endorsement
of the multiple substance view of nature that goes beyond the
position of the chemists. The issue would seem confused, but there
is more confusion to come.

The philosophic reader will be well aware that some
philosophers claim there is no substance at all. We shall let one of
them, in a well known piece, speak for the group:

> According to what we may call the substratum
> theory, a thing such as an apple or a pebble is
> composed of a substance in which a variety of

attributes inhere, or which supports them or is their
bearer or their owner. The substance itself is held to
be something distinct from the sum of its properties.
It is also held that our "experience" of a thing is
confined to its qualities, so that it is possible for us to
know what attributes the thing has; but what the
possessor of the attributes, the substratum itself, is,
remains hidden from us . . . .

Not all philosophers have been able to accept this
theory. Instead, some have been attracted to a
different view about the composition of physical
things, one from which it follows that there are no
unknowable substances. This view is to the effect
that a thing is composed of nothing more than the
properties which, in ordinary language, "it" is said to
have: "What would commonly be called a 'thing' is
nothing but a bundle of coexisting qualities such as
hardness, redness, etc." [The quotation is from
Bertrand Russell.] On this theory we can know what
things really are, because there are no substances
distinct from the experienceable qualities.[5]

Commonly those who deny substance grant that qualities are real,
but say that qualities do not require an unperceivable, unknowable
substratum in which to reside, on account of which what we call
"things" are "bundles" of qualities. As for the non-existent
substance we spontaneously talk about, some would hold that it is
an illusion of language, and Lazerowitz puts the blame on
metaphysicians for having deceived us:

I propose to take the view . . . that the substance
"theory" is only the verbal imitation of a theory and
entirely different from what we are inclined to think
it is. But I shall argue that it is not ordinary,
everyday language that causes us to think this.
Instead, I shall try to show that the illusion of its
being a theory about things is produced by a
concealed *revision* of ordinary subject-predicate form
of discourse itself. It is what *metaphysicians*

[emphasis his] have done with words, their metaphysical artistry, that creates the appearance of a theory about the structure of things; but what they have done is hidden from our conscious awareness, as well as their own. The theory may be compared to a dream; in this case, the metaphysician may be said to dream with words.[6]

As we know, for some time it was fashionable to consider much in philosophy as a kind of nonsense invented by metaphysicians. Yet no matter how we account for our ordinary way of speaking, the denial of substance as a reality is an issue that is separate from why ordinary language indicates we accept it; for the latter question presupposes as true that there is no substance. So we shall ask the first question directly: does a substance exist? Other problems that have arisen in connection with the topic cannot be taken up until this first question is answered.

Notes to Chapter 1

[1]The quotation is representative; but see William Nebergall, Frederic C. Schmidt, Henry F. Holtzclaw Jr., *College Chemistry* (Lexington, Massachusetts: D. C. Heath and Company, 1976), p. 5.

[2]Ibid.

[3]Albert Einstein and Leopold Infeld, *The Evolution of Physics* (New York: Simon and Schuster, 1954), p. 208.

[4]Edward O. Dodson, *Evolution: Process and Product* (New York: Rheinhold Publishing Company, 1960), p. 54.

[5]Morris Lazerowitz, "Substratum," *Philosophical Analysis*, ed. Max Black (Englewood Cliffs, N.J.: Prentice-Hall, Inc., 1963), pp. 166-183.

[6]Ibid.

CHAPTER 2

SUBSTANCE

A. Preliminaries

The Oxford English Dictionary traces a long history of the word "thing," but in the ordinary language of our time it signifies "Whatever can be perceived, known, or thought to have a separate existence; an entity."[1] The term "entity" points to the sense the word "thing" has when philosophers wish to discuss things and thing-words; so when we check "entity" under its own entry we find: "A particular and discrete unit; an entirety."[2] This listing indicates the most relevant features of things or entities, namely, their individual character as units and as wholes. Dogs and ants are things; so are oak trees and water lilies.

The whole of the reality encompassed within the limits of observation is called the "universe," and lexicographers tell us "universe" signifies "All existing things, including the earth, the heavens, the galaxies, and all therein, regarded as a whole: the cosmos, the macrocosm."[3] The most common, minimal description we can give of the universe is that it is the collection of natural things taken as a whole; consequently when viewed as a unit-whole, it too is a thing. *Whole*, of course, implies *parts*, for in ordinary usage the word "whole" signifies "Containing all component parts; complete... ."[4] Still, in our first understanding of

a whole we do not see clearly or distinctly the nature of its parts;
our first grasp of things as wholes is indistinct or confused.

Our ordinary experience tells us the universe can be divided
into two main parts,the heavens and the earth. The larger of the
parts contains things called "constellations," which in turn contain
other things called "stars." The earth, too, contains parts that are
things, such as oceans, continents, mountains; and these are
habitats for other things, namely plants and animals. Furthermore, when we take advantage of what modern science teaches us,
we know that all these things, too, have their own thing-parts,
down to the elementary particles. These last are simple things, not
composed as are the wholes they constitute.

But we cannot speak about the common notion of *thing* without
also speaking about the common notion of *stuff*. In ordinary usage
"stuff" signifies "The material out of which something is made or
formed; substance."[5] The common notion of *material* is indeterminate in the sense that it does not specify whether the stuff is one
or many. Stuff is "Material not specifically identified,"[6] or as
Webster's (second edition) has it, stuff is "any material, substance,
or aggregation of matter, regarded indefinitely; as lava is curious
stuff." Hence the word signifies *things* insofar as they contain a
material or materials, a substance or substances, out of which they
are made. Put more accurately, when the word "stuff" is taken
formally it signifies something *insofar as it is that out of which
another is made*, although we also use the word when stuffs are not
explicitly viewed in relation to the thing they compose. At such
times "stuff" is equivalent to "substance," for even to chemists
"substance" does not uniformly imply a material composing
something else, though the chemist's substances are such
materials and even though they are often discovered by analysis of
composites. In sum, then, *things* are conceived as unit realities or
entities, some of which are composed of other things, and all of
which contain some *stuff* or *stuffs*.

When we speak of things or the stuffs of which they are made,
we speak of them as having *properties*, some of which are
conditions, states, etc. They are admittedly real, for those who deny
the reality of a substance-substratum are at pains to declare that
properties or qualities are the only true realities. There are, to be
sure, many kinds of properties. Things or stuffs are said to be
solid, liquid, gaseous, gray, sweet, hard, soft, viscous, conductive,
elastic, etc., and such properties are the concern of physics and

chemistry. At the moment, however, we need not consider their multiplicity and variety; all we need is the acknowledgment that properties are real, whether substances are or not. So with these uses of terms in mind, we shall undertake our consideration of substance by starting from the statement "*Properties* (qualities) *are real.*"

B. Properties: what they are

As we ordinarily use the word "real" it is opposed to "non-real," "fictitious," or "imaginary." Furthermore, the notion of *the real* or *reality* is primitive, even absolutely primitive, for there is nothing prior to it in the mind's conceptions.[7] The real, then, is *that which exists outside the mind and imagination,* which means that existence distinguishes the real. The phrase "outside the mind and the imagination" is of course redundant and a circumlocution, but it is added to make the sense of "real" as clear as possible. Though the real can exist in the mind or imagination, it does not exist *only* there, whereas if the non-real, fictitious, or imaginary "exists" in any sense, it exists *only* in the mind or imagination; and used that way, the word "exist" has received an extended sense. In short, the distinction between existence and non-existence is the primitive distinction. But now to properties.

Observation shows that some properties vary while others remain the same. When an animal or any other body moves from one place to another, its location varies but its other properties do not. Similarly, a lump of clay can undergo a change of shape without undergoing changes in its color, density, etc. In each of these instances one reality varies while others remain the same. But more importantly, after the changes have been completed there is "more" that is unmodified in the animal and the clay than there are differences that have been introduced.

We see in ourselves the most obvious case in which one reality varies while something else remains. We are all aware that we-- whatever *we* may be--stay the same in every important respect when we go from here to there, or when we change our position from sitting to standing. Even when we grow from a child to an adult "much" in us remains unmodified. But let us examine a change in a property to see what is entailed.

A piece of clay has many properties and, when it undergoes a change of shape, its texture, mass, plasticity, etc., remain unvaried. As a consequence, the principle of non-contradiction requires us to distinguish the shape that varies from the properties that do not vary. Further considerations make us realize that shape always exists in conjunction with something else; shape never occurs in complete isolation. Something always has the shape, which is said to be in the something. Furthermore, we know that shape is the limit or boundary where "something else" leaves off. Looking at ourselves, we readily confirm that our shape is the boundary where "we" leave off and that it is in us. So we can define shape as *that which exists in another as in a subject*; and insofar as it exists in another, it is dependent on that other. Nor is the phrase "as in a subject" a superfluous part of the formula, for by it the relevant meaning of "in" is distinguished from the meanings that are not relevant. One reality can be in another in many ways: as a hat is in a closet, as an effect is in a cause, as a cause is in an effect, as a part is in a whole, as a whole is in its parts, etc. Hence the formula shows the way in which shape exists in another.

But the definition does not belong to shape alone, for it can also be applied to magnitude, elasticity, conductivity, motion, etc. In short, the definition obtained from shape *fits properties commonly*. Stated another way, if we were to call some reality a "property" that did not fit the definition, the name would have been extended and would require a second definition.

It will be recognized that the kind of reality we have called "property" the medieval philosophers called *accidens*, usually translated into English as "accident." Of course "accidental" does not mean "incidental" or "contingent," although some accidents do belong contingently to their subjects. Nor does it mean "fortuitous" or "by chance." But since "contingent" and "by chance" are part of the usual understanding of "accident," we prefer to use the term "property," which does not imply either contingency or fortuitousness.

C. Substance: what it is

Having touched on the nature of properties, we must now ask about the subject in which they exist. If shape, for instance, exists in another as in a subject, then does the subject too exist in another as in a subject? It might very well, for shape exists in a magnitude and motion in a shaped magnitude. But then how far can this dependence on a subject go? Does the second subject exist in another, and that in another ad infinitum? The regress, however, cannot go on infinitely; hence we must *infer* that *something exists that does not require a subject,* and we call this "substance." Substance, then, is *that which exists in itself* (or by itself) *and not in another as in a subject.* Plainly this is a minimal notion which does no more than delineate a basic distinction implicitly recognized on the basis of ordinary experience.

The argument above concludes to the existence of a substance by denying an infinite regress; yet even were that to be disputed, the reality of substance is evident. We know empirically that things exist separately from each other. Chipmunks are separate from and independent of black bears and oak trees; the earth is separate from and independent of the moon, and so on. Again we ourselves are the most obvious instances, for we do not reside in the earth, the atmosphere, or any other reality as in a subject. This means that we as well as other things are either substances or aggregates of them. To repeat the point: no observation or other kind of evidence permits us to maintain that a man is related to a horse or to any other thing the way shape is to magnitude or motion to a billiard ball. It seems, then, that substance is a reality which plays the role of substratum; it "stands under" properties.

D. Substance: what it is not

Having seen that something must exist by itself and that we call this "substance," we are in a position to note that substance does not imply either an unqualified permanence or an unqualified independence. Though substance is permanent in relation to physical changes, the definition at which we have arrived does not imply permanence in an absolute sense. That is, from the definition we cannot conclude that substance neither comes to be nor passes away in nature. Kant, therefore, is not justified in claiming that the permanent qua permanent is the substratum; for even if substances cease to be, while they exist they are substrata for properties.[8] Similarly, though substances are independent of subjects for their existence, that kind of independence is in no way absolute. We have no grounds at present for claiming that

substance is independent in the sense of being uncaused with no
need of anything else to exist, as Descartes would have it.   If
permanence and independence are to be assigned to substance in
an unqualified way, they will have to be assigned through
arguments or else postulated a priori as part of some hypothesis or
theory.

Another point to be made is that the definition we have
obtained in no way implies that substance is simple and cannot be
composed, though many persons do tend to assume that that is the
case, as we see in Leibniz' *Monadology*:

1. The Monad, of which we will speak here, is nothing else
   than a simple substance, which goes to make up
   composites; by simple we mean without parts.
2. There must be simple substances because there are
   composites; for a composite is nothing else than a collection
   or aggregatum of simple substances.[9]

(Leibniz actually begs the question in arguing to the existence of
simple substances.) The unwarranted assumption he makes about
the simplicity of substance is also made by a contemporary author:

> A "living" substance has often been spoken of.
> This concept is due to a fundamental fallacy. There
> is no "living substance" in the sense that lead, water,
> or cellulose are substances, where any arbitrarily
> taken part shows the same properties as the rest.
> Rather is life bound to individualized and organized
> systems, the destruction of which puts an end to it.[10]

Organisms cannot be substances, this author says, for organisms
have heterogeneous parts. Substances, he believes, are homogeneous, every part like every other part. Although a truly
elementary particle is undoubtedly a substance, from what we
know so far, any statement that claims substance is necessarily
simple is gratuitous; whether that is or is not so is one of the
principal issues to be considered in this book.

The last point we wish to make here is that the problem about
the existence of substance ought not to be identified with the

problem of individuation. We do concede that individual things which are substances--some individual things are not--are substances in the fullest sense of the word. Yet individuals may be considered according to that which they have in common, according to that which is signified by the definition, and our discussion of substance will concern itself with this common nature. The problem of individuation can be properly considered only after one knows more about substance. Furthermore, although time and position (in the sense of location) are the identifying marks of individuals, we cannot say that position is substance, as Anthony Quinton seems to do.[11] Position is a property of a subject; there is no position except there be a thing positioned; position does not exist by itself. But let us leave these general considerations and turn to David Hume; for though Locke began the attack on substance, Hume is mainly responsible for the negative views of our day.

E. Essentials of the argument recapitulated

1. Definition: property is that which exists in another as in a subject.
2. Disjunctive argument:
    a. Every property exists in an infinitely regressing series of subjects or in something that does not require a subject;
    b. but no property exists in an infinitely regressing series of subjects;
    c. therefore every property exists in something that does not require a subject.
3. Definition: substance is that which exists in itself (by itself) and not in another as in a subject.

Notes to Chapter 2

[1] *The American Heritage Dictionary of the English Language.*

2Ibid.

3Ibid.

4Ibid.

5Ibid.

6Ibid.

7*Non-real* plainly cannot be understood if *real* is not; the same can be said of anything that is understood as a negation--either wholly or partially--of something else. Hence no negation can be an absolutely primitive notion.

8*Critique of Pure Reason*, trans. Norman Kemp Smith (London: Macmillan & Co., Ltd., 1956), pp. 212ff., also p. 229.

9*Leibniz*, trans. George R. Montgomery (LaSalle, Illinois: The Open Court Publishing Co., 1962), p. 251.

10Ludwig Von Bertalanffy, *Problems of Life* (New York: John Wiley and Sons, Inc., 1952), p. 13.

11*The Nature of Things* (London: Routledge & Kegan Paul, 1972).

CHAPTER 3

HUME ON SUBSTANCE

A. Hume's view

Writing in his *Treatise*, David Hume denounced the notion of substance, and he did so without blush or apology:

> We have, therefore, no idea of substance, distinct from that of a collection of particular qualities, nor have we any other meaning when we either talk or reason concerning it. The idea of substance as well as that of a mode is nothing but a collection of simple ideas, that are united by the imagination, and have a particular name assigned them, by which we are able to recall, either to ourselves or others, that collection. But the difference betwixt these ideas consists in this, that the particular qualities, which form a substance, are commonly referr'd to as an unknown *something*, in which they are supposed to be closely and inseparately connected by the relations of contiguity and causation.[1]

Hume claims we have no idea of substance as a substratum but only as a collection of qualities; and as we might expect, his view of properties--accidents--is affected:

> The notion of *accidents* is an unavoidable consequence of this method of thinking with regard to substances or substantial forms: nor can we forbear looking upon colours, sounds, tastes, figures, and other properties of bodies, as existences, which cannot subsist apart, but require a subject of inhesion to sustain and support them. For having never discover'd any of these sensible qualities, where, for the reasons above mention'd, we did not likewise fancy a substance to exist; the same habit, which makes us infer a connection betwixt cause and effect, makes us here infer a dependence of every quality on the unknown substance. The custom of imagining a dependence has the same effect as the custom of observing it wou'd have. This conceit, however, is no more reasonable than any of the foregoing. Every quality being a distinct thing from another, may be conceiv'd to exist apart, and may exist apart not only from every other quality, but from that unintelligible chimera of a substance.[2]

Here Hume tells us that the properties of bodies are only imagined to exist in a substratum; they have no such dependence in reality. Assigning them to a substratum is but a habit of mind, on account of which we may say that the qualities we observe are rightly conceived to exist apart, "not only from every other quality, but from that unintelligible chimera of a substance." But he has more to say.

The reader will recall that on several occasions in chapter 2 we spoke of ourselves as subjects of properties on the ground that whatever "we" may be, either we are or we contain a substance or substances. This means that the *self* in some way or another is substantial, and as one might expect, Hume's doctrine of personal identity reflects his denial of substance. He notes that some philosophers (not to mention the plain man) think they have an

idea of self, and to this he sets himself in opposition on the
following grounds:

> It must be some one impression that gives rise to
> every real idea. But self or person is not any one
> impression, but that to which our several
> impressions and ideas are supposed to have a
> reference. If any impression gives rise to the idea of
> self, that impression must continue invariably the
> same, thro' the whole course of our lives; since self is
> suppos'd to exist after that manner. But here is no
> impression constant and invariable. . . .
> But farther, what must become of all our
> particular perceptions upon this hypothesis? All
> these are different, and distinguishable, and
> separable from each other, and may be separately
> consider'd, and may exist separately, and have no
> need of anything to support their existence.[3]

One does not know himself, we are told, as an individual substance,
which means that "self" cannot be taken to signify a substratum-
substance. And though one might take Hume to be talking about
ideas or concepts, we shall construe him to be talking about
realities; that is, we shall take him to deny the reality of substance,
not just our ability to conceive it; for that is the issue with which we
are concerned, and the one current in philosophy. But in either
case, whether we talk about concepts or realities, Hume's position
leads to absurdities; and we shall now see what some of them are.

Suppose for the moment that Hume is right: qualities do not
require a substratum, and qualities are real; they exist outside the
knower but not in a substratum. From this we obviously get his
position that qualities cannot be properties or accidents as we have
defined them. To restate his position: if qualities exist, and if they
do not exist in a substratum, *then they exist in themselves and not in
another as in a subject.* Thus because there is no third alternative
(something either exists or does not exist in a subject), Hume has
turned qualities into substances. Without realizing it, he has
actually endorsed the notion of substance first delineated by
Aristotle and, contrary to his words, he has actually denied the

20   Chapter 3

reality of properties *as such*. In sum, Hume has turned all qualities and thus all realities into substances. But we must do him justice, for he appears to take what we have just now said into account. In another passage he tells us:

> If . . . anyone should say that the definition of a substance is *something which may exist by itself*: and that this definition ought to satisfy us: Shou'd this be said, I shou'd observe, that this definition agrees to everything, that can possibly be conceiv'd; and never will serve to distinguish substance from accident, or the soul from its perceptions. For thus I reason. Whatever is clearly conceiv'd may exist; and whatever is clearly conceiv'd, after any manner, may exist after the same manner. This is one principle, which has been already acknowledg'd. Again, every thing, which is different, is distinguishable, and every thing which is distinguishable, is separable by the imagination. This is another principle. My conclusion from both is, that since all our perceptions are different from each other, and from every thing else in the universe, they are also distinct and separable, and may be consider'd as separately existent, and may exist separately, as the definition explains a substance.[4]

It would appear that Hume is willing to live with the implication of his position, for he says, "this definition agrees to everything." Everything is a substance; there are no properties. But given what he has said, Hume ought to have tried to account for our observations, since our sensations themselves are the first ground for our recognizing that *in some way* the set of properties we observe in a stuff is not separable. That there is some principle of their unity in reality cannot be questioned; we cannot say their union is only noetic.

But not only is the position he takes not in accord with observation, his fundamental premiss is untenable: "Whatever is clearly conceived may exist; and whatever is clearly conceived, after any manner, may exist after that same manner." The untenable character of this proposition is well known to philosophers, so we shall forbear comment on it.

It is also plain that Hume has equivocated on "exist by itself," and his argument is fallacious on that account. This phrase can mean "separately from other properties," that is, meaning that one property is separable from another because it can exist in two things which do not have the same set of accompanying properties. But it can also mean "not in a subject," and though a property can exist by itself in the first sense, it cannot in the second. With that, let us now make some applications of Hume's position to real things.

If things are collections of qualities-become-substances, then these things are themselves collections of other things. A quality-substance would have to be an individual entity, for something subsisting that has its own character and is divided off from other realities is what an individual is. Hence, any thing described by a collection of qualities would be an aggregate of substances.

To pursue the point in a somewhat different way, let us suppose that the magnitude, the shape and the motion of a billiard ball are qualities-become-substances. It would then follow that the motion of the ball must be distinct and separate from the shape and the magnitude, and that the three individuals must be united to each other exteriorly; that is, the motion must be united to the shape and to the magnitude in the way in which an arm is joined to the body or one freight car to another. The only other possible mode of union would be for one quality-substance to interpenetrate the others. That, however, is impossible, for two or more qualities united as interpenetrating substances would be identical. To put it another way, whatever differences they had would not be distinguishable. Furthermore, if the motion is independent of the magnitude and its shape, then what happens when the ball moves? Does the individual motion pull the individual-shape and the individual-magnitude along like appendages? If so, then the shape and the magnitude move too, and there is not one motion but three; or rather, the number of motions is one plus another number equal to the number of quality-substances. Obviously, too, every motion but the first will reside in other qualities and will be properties of them. On the other hand, if the motion does not pull the shape and magnitude along, then the shape and magnitude on one hand and the motion on the other must become constantly more separated; thus the ball as a whole could hardly be said to move. But though

the absurdity of both of these alternatives is obvious, both of them
follow from the supposition that in reality qualities do not inhere in
a subject and are independent entities.

And so we must conclude that Hume did not reflect clearly on
what he said. He did not pay enough attention to the implications,
simple though they are, of his denial of a substratum. Certainly
the unity of magnitude, shape, and motion in a single real thing
cannot be explained if they do not reside in another as in a subject.
And let it be emphasized that we cannot acquire the notion of
subject without an observed union of properties. We *see* the *shaped
magnitude moving*; all is observed simultaneously in a union. It
would seem that Hume's position is anything but empirical.

B. Views of others: the same error

It might appear that the modern denial of substance could take
many forms and that there might be some alternative to the bundle
theory proclaimed by Hume. H. H. Price seems to suggest that is so
when he says:

> We may distinguish between two different ways of
> looking at the universe, two contrasted metaphysical
> "world views." On the one hand, you may think of
> the world in the way Aristotle did, as composed of
> substances or things, *res per se subsistentes*; and then
> an event is something which happens to or in a
> substance, and a particular is either itself a
> substance or else it is a state of some substance. On
> the other hand, you may think of the universe as
> Russell, Whitehead, and the Buddhists do. Then you
> will hold that events or temporally-brief particulars
> are the ultimate constituents of the world, and that
> the notion of substance or thinghood is both impre-
> cise and derivative. On this view what is referred to
> by a thing-word such as "cat" or "tree" is a complex
> series of events or temporally-brief particulars,
> related to each other by relations of temporal and/or
> spatial continuity and by certain sorts of inductively

establishable rules of sequence, sometimes called
rules of "immanent causality."[5]

Substances or events: these are the alternatives, says Price. If one
rejects substance, then a thing such as a cat is a complex series of
events or temporally-brief particulars. Considered under its most
general aspect, Price has described the process philosophy view of
the world, and he also has suggested that the two ways of looking
at it are a matter of option. No settling of the issue seems possible;
at least that is what his remarks and the general practice both
seem to indicate.

But those who hold that events or processes rather than
things--whatever the character of the events and processes--are the
fundamental realities, must face the same alternatives as Hume.
As long as an event, movement, process, etc., whether
psychological or physical, is held to have a real existence, then
either it exists in a subject or it does not. But as with other
properties, an event or process that exists without a subject is a
substance. From the point of view of their mode of existence, such
realities are not different from non-event, non-process, non-motion
properties. And plainly, if events are fundamental and do not
belong to subjects, then the universe is Heraclitean in the full
sense of "all is flux."

Furthermore, a process view cannot escape professing a bundle
theory. The difference is that the members of the bundle which
constitute the "derivative" thing simply have become events or
processes instead of "static" properties, so it would seem that Hume
spoke for all who deny the reality of substance.

As a last comment, I would like to note that substance is not a
theoretical notion in the sense that it can be taken as an
assumption; that is, the statement "Substance is a substratum for
properties" is not an hypothesis. The reader will recognize that our
argument depended on the impossibility of contradiction, which
means that necessarily there is at least one substance in nature.

C. Essentials of the argument recapitulated

1. Hume's position:
   a. qualities are real (this must be granted or there is no argument at all);
   b. qualities do not exist in a substratum;
   c. therefore since qualities fulfill the definition of substance, they are all substances.
   d. The reality of properties has actually been denied.
2. Hume's position fails:
   a. because if every reality were a substance, one reality could not modify another, as does shape the clay or motion the ball; and
   b. the observed unity of properties cannot be explained.

Notes to Chapter 3

[1]*A Treatise of Human Nature*, ed. Selby-Bigge (Oxford: The Clarendon Press, 1975), p. 16.

[2]Ibid., p. 222.

[3]Ibid., p. 251.

[4]Ibid., p. 233.

[5]"Appearing and Appearances," *American Philosophical Quarterly*, Vol. I, No. 1, January, 1964.

CHAPTER 4

CATEGORIES AND KINDS OF THINGS

A. Categories

Once we have distinguished substance from property, we can formulate a theory of categories that is founded on realities. Modern philosophy has tended to view categories as a matter of choice, which means that they are regarded as arbitrary. When one classifies the products of human manufacture, he does indeed have some choice in putting them into "categories." Classifications of artefactual entities are not fixed but are ordinarily a matter of convenience and so in that sense arbitrary. (Note: I shall use the coined word "artefactual" in place of "artificial" because the latter too often has the sense of "fictitious," corresponding to the philosophical use of "artifact" for "fiction.") The realm of the artefactual, of things made by the fine arts, the mechanical arts, and the engineering sciences, is a realm apart from nature. Considered most commonly, the artefactual is *that which is produced by human intelligence and volition*, which means that men determine the character, the "nature," of all such entities. And because men modify them as they will, the classifications of artefacts are not fixed. On the other hand, the natural, considered most commonly, is *that which is not dependent on human intelligence and volition*; natural things can come to be without us, so this common definition is negative. Consequently, when we speak about categories here, we speak about *categories of natural things and properties*. Any utility the categories might have for dealing with artefacts is very limited and secondary to their utility for natural classifications. On that account, the substance-property distinction we have justified precludes holding that the distinction of ultimate genera, of categories, is arbitrary. Substance is the primary reality and the primary category, whereas properties are secondary realities and secondary categories. Furthermore, properties themselves are of several distinct ultimate genera. A beaver has a size that is not the same as his shape or his pliability or his location or his paternity, etc.; and the latter properties are not the same as each other. And though our aim is not to give a complete enumeration and defense of a system of categories, we nonetheless need to recognize some distinctions among them. The magnitude of a thing or the amount of some stuff is *quantity*, pliability is a *quality*, in the sea is a *location*, paternity is a *relation*; etc. Thus, the categories are distinct from one another, a sign of which is that we cannot say quality is a quantity, or a location, etc. One category cannot be predicated of any other. But again, the precise way in which properties of all kinds are determinations of substance is the business of category theory, a business we are not required to enter upon here.

Perhaps we ought to note that many qualities can be varied in degree; they can be found in things and stuff according to a more or less, as for instance warmth, viscosity, and conductivity. When we seek to measure the intensity of such properties, when we seek to measure their degree, we make what we call "quantitative determinations" of the qualities themselves; but such determinations often are not of the *amount* or *quantity* of the thing or stuff. In other words, "quantitative difference," a term essential to the natural sciences, refers to any difference of more or less, whether the difference be one of quantity or some other property. At this point, however, we need not press the issue further.

B. Kinds of things: (1) non-substance-things or property-things

As we said, the category of substance and the several categories of properties pertain to natural entities; consequently, artefactual entities cannot be classified by means of them. Neither a table, a chair, a spoon, nor any other artefact can be properly categorized as a substance, although some persons are inclined to so categorize them. If we ask what gives artefacts their "species," their "kinds," we must reply that they are characterized by the forms which human intelligence imposes upon natural materials. A statue has a determinate shape through which it becomes a representation of Socrates, say, and the shape or figure determines its "species," as is true also of tables and chairs. The more complicated artefacts, such as automobiles and computers, *ultimately* receive their character from the order (the structure or arrangement) according to which the many differentiated parts are assembled. But the point is this: names such as "table" and "machine" signify a material or materials that are determined by a property, and it is the property that the name directly and immediately manifests, however much the property cannot exist without the materials, and however much the latter are indirectly included in the significations of the names. Hence that which is composed in this way and taken *as such* (the property as determining the materials) *cannot go in one category*. The shape of the statue goes in the category quality and the wood (we shall assume for the moment that it is a substance, not an aggregate of substances) goes in another, namely substance, but the *shaped wood* cannot go in *one* category. Likewise, the structure of the machine is an ordering and is in the category of relation, whereas the materials go elsewhere. And we may repeat these comments for every other artefact.

The same point can be made in connection with some classes of natural things. A *white rabbit* certainly cannot go in one category, for *white* is a quality but *rabbit* is not. This example is obvious because of its complex name, "white rabbit," but some composite things are more obscure because they are signified by single names. "Grammarian (a person who knows grammar)" is a case in point, for we cannot put what it signifies in one category. Nor can we do this with "boulder (large stone)" or "planet." Although the latter is a single body, it is an ordered aggregate of stuffs which together make up a whole. There are, of course, instances of other classes that are determined by properties. A basketball team, a legislature, a city, an army, a galaxy--all are specified by a property, however true it is that the substances which the properties order or modify are the "more important" realities.

Yet we sometimes do speak of *table*, for example, and other artefactual things as though they were in the category of substance. We do the same with *boulder* and *grammarian*. But when we do, we put them there by reason of the wood of the table, the minerals of the boulder, etc., and not by reason of anything else. In short, we categorize them as substances by reason of their stuffs, and by ignoring the specifying properties signified by the names. It is important to be aware of the nature of the practice, for artefacts cannot properly be classified as substances.

On the other hand, when we categorize artefacts *according to their artefactual character*, we actually classify properties, chief of which is the function, even though the properties cannot exist without the materials. We might add that the function accounts for most of the other properties (some are merely concomitant with those that are desired) except, perhaps, the properties that address our esthetic sensibilities. In short, an artefact is both specified and individualized through the actions of human causes, and it is what we shall call a "property-thing."

As we have said, some natural things, such as planets, stars, galaxies, etc., are characterized by a property that determines a collection of natural stuffs, and we shall call them "property-things" also. When man is subdivided into cultural, ethnic, racial, psychological, or similar groups, and when other organisms are subdivided into varieties, the realities that distinguish races and cultures and varieties are properties which do not constitute species. We would not, however, call races, varieties, etc. property-things because the properties that determine them are subordinated to established biological species that have already been classified. But we have said enough to make our point clear, so we shall not pursue this topic further.

C. Kinds of things: (2) substance-things

Physicists hold the ultimate constituents of the universe to be elementary particles, for instance, electrons or photons, and they are conceived as substances. Even photons are to be taken as things because they are held to be quanta of energy that do not exist in something else as in a subject. So *whatever their nature or description*, truly elementary particles do not derive their character as units from a property imposed upon an antecedently existing stuff that can "take the property or leave it." Hence elementary particles must be substance-things. Whether there are other substance-things must, however, be argued later.

CHAPTER 5

THE PROBLEM RECONSIDERED

A. Introduction

Anthony Quinton opens his book on things with the comment that "substance is the oldest topic of philosophical inquiry and it is also one of the most entangled."[1] His remark is certainly true; and if we are to consider this oldest of topics, we shall have to untangle some of its threads. Therefore let us begin by stating what we did in the previous chapters and then follow up by comparing it to what Aristotle did. He was the first to consider substance extensively, and his writings probably occasioned most of the entanglements.

B. Substance and ordinary experience

Our first four chapters centered on the question whether there is a substance. We answered it by deriving a definition of *property* from observable data, and then we presented an argument to show that property itself implies the existence of another kind of reality that is subjectless. Although the argument concluded necessarily, it did no more than identify substance by its most common characteristic. The definition is accurate as far as it goes, but it does not provide a complete understanding of substance and its properties.   On that account, what we know so far is only preliminary to fuller considerations; but we must elaborate.

Up to now our considerations have only made explicit what is implicit in ordinary experience and signified in ordinary language. Hence the notion of substance we have delineated is not properly part of a philosophical system or theory. As with any human discipline, a philosophy that is systematic has to be grounded on ordinary experience; yet when we reflect on and define objects of ordinary experience we are not within a system, however carefully argued our position may be. We can be systematic, so to speak, without having a system.[2] Now many of Aristotle's considerations on substance took place within his system, and that, I would suggest, has been the occasion of some confusions. So with that in mind, let us take an abbreviated look at what Aristotle did in order to distinguish better our common consideration from those that are within a system.[3] As we suggested, the failure to see these distinctions probably accounts for many of the entanglements.

C. Aristotle and substance

Aristotle's considerations on substance in the *Categoriae*[4] are logical in the sense that he there takes up substance insofar as it has logical properties--relational properties--that belong to it in the mind but not in reality. An Aristotelian would say that logic treats the order of concepts or mental processes with a view to determining the legitimacy of arguments and definitions. That is not, however, an endorsement of psychologism. Logic is not a part of psychology, nor is it grounded on a priori forms of thought. Because the intelligence has its own nature, when realities are conceived they are present in it according to the conditions proper to the intelligence itself. The medievals made this clear by applying a very general proposition: "Quidquid recipitur ad modum recipientis recipitur (whatever is received is received according to the mode--the measure, the condition, the limits--of the receiver)." So given the truth of that proposition, our conceptions of realities will have to be related to one another according to their condition in the mind. Indisputably, arguments, definitions, and their parts are in the mind and, indisputably, realities do not exist in nature in the same way they do in the mind. In other words, the mental order cannot be regarded as isomorphic with reality, as a mapping of the real world on the intelligence. Thus an order in the mind and an order in reality belong to different domains and cannot be embraced in one and the same consideration. But let us make the point at issue more specifically.

Aristotle defines substance in the *Categoriae* as "that which does not exist in a subject and is not predicable of a subject,"[5] a formula that adds the property of predicability to the definition we presented earlier; and this definition is said to be *logical*. As given, it fits individuals, for the latter neither exist in a subject nor are predicable of a subject. Predicability is a property realities have in the mind, but it does not belong to individuals. (When I say "That man is John," I attach a name to the man; but predicability, Aristotelians claim, belongs to that which is conceived as common.)[6] On the other hand, the nature substances share that is apprehended by the mind as common is predicable of individuals even though it does not exist in a subject. This Aristotle called "second substance"; the former he called "first substance." So whether the Aristotelians are right or wrong, this consideration of substance is within the system.

From this we can see that Aristotle's treatment of substance in the *Categoriae* ought not to be confused with the notion we defended from common experience; for the properties of predicability, of being a middle term, etc., belongs to things in their mental status but not in nature. It should also be plain that considerations on how the mind orders its concepts are not the business of psychology. The only common ground logic and psychology have is that each in its own way deals with the intelligence; so it seems simplistic to say that logic must not make references to mental activities on the ground that it would be invading the territory of psychology.

In Book I of his *Physica*, Aristotle treats substance with the aim of showing its constituting principles. He thought this necessary because he maintained that natural substances come to be and pass away. Later, in his *De Generatione et Corruptione*, Aristotle again treats the coming to be and passing away of substances, primarily the production and destruction of those that are elementary. But in those two books substance is considered according to the status it has in reality; both books are part of the Aristotelian science of the natural world.

Finally, let us note that we must not confuse any of the foregoing considerations with the treatment of substance in the

Metaphysica, which presupposes not only what has been done in the *Categoriae* but more especially what has been done in the *Physica.* Additionally, the *Metaphysica* presupposes for the questions proper to it that substances are of two generically different kinds: physical and non-physical. Its special aim is to treat the principles of both, making clear, nonetheless, the different ways properties are causally related to the two kinds of substance. And because those that are physical are more accessible to us they provide an analogy for considering those that are not physical.

In sum, substance can be the object of a number of different considerations, and the one we undertook in our first four chapters is an explication of the notions of ordinary experience that are presupposed to every systematic study of nature. In the chapters that follow, however, what we shall do belongs properly to the systematic philosophy of natural entities.

D. Substance and the formation of hypotheses

Our last point repeats one we have already made: the propositions "Substance exists" and "Properties exist in substances," as well as others like them, are not hypotheses. They are not assumptions accepted or rejected only on the basis of their ability to account either for what we observe or for our linguistic behavior. The truth of the claim is evident from the earlier procedures through which we defined *property* on empirical grounds and then inferred the existence of substance from the definition. So if what we did was legitimate, the notions of *property* and *substance* are not assumptions and hence not hypotheses. Either we have established them apodictically or we have done nothing.

E. The problems to come

Having determined that there is a substance, the question arises as to whether there is more than one in nature. Is the chemist right in claiming that chemical change is a change of substance? and the biologist in claiming that protoplasm is yet a different substance?

It would be reasonable for a theory of matter to *postulate* that elementary particles are not only individual substances but that they also differ in kind.   The question most properly arises, however, about the substantive character of macroscopic entities; and when we address it in its most general form, the possible answers are two: macroscopic entities are either *substance-things* (more briefly, *substances*) or *property-things*.   Faced with these alternatives, the mechanist would immediately reply that every thing other than the elementary substance-particles is an ordered collection or arrangement of particles; that is, a property-thing. Those who take the mechanistic position claim the support of contemporary physical theory, and if their view is right, then mechanism (or reductionism) becomes the only sound philosophy of natural entities.   More particularly, although biological activities appear to constitute their own genus, in fact they could be no more than some particular organization of physical and chemical processes.   In principle if not in practice, every biological activity would have to be accounted for by the laws of physics and chemistry. The difficulties we encounter would be the result of our lack of understanding and could be expected to disappear in the future.

On the other hand, if we are not entitled to say that all macroscopic entities are property-things, then some at least are substances, which means that there is more than one substance in nature. Difficulties about the knowability of substances arise, too, especially in view of the claim that they would be bare particulars.

And so in the chapters of Part II that follow we shall (1) describe some ancient views about the nature of macroscopic things; (2) describe some modern and contemporary views about the nature of things; (3) describe machines to see whether they are a kind of model for organisms; (4) consider whether chemical compounds are property-things (aggregates); (5) consider whether organisms are property-things (aggregates); (6) consider the kind of relation that exists among the activities of organisms; (7) consider the internal constituting principles of natural substances. Other questions, those about the knowability of substances, will be treated while we are discussing the issues above.

Notes to Chapter 5

1The Nature of Things (London and Boston: Routledge & Kegan Paul, 1973).

2Perhaps I should note that although we might identify Ordinary Language Philosophy as a "school" or "philosophical movement," I do not think we would speak of it as "system," which would tend to confirm our point about philosophical reflections on ordinary experience being properly pre-systematic.

3The remarks we make here about the differences in Aristotle's treatment of substance are essentially the views of medieval philosophy, especially Thomas Aquinas.

4The names we use here are in their Latin form; we are merely following the practice of the Oxford edition of *The Works of Aristotle.*

5The Oxford edition of *The Works of Aristotle,* Vol. I, 1a, 30, reads as follows: "There is . . . a class of things which are neither present in a subject nor predicable of a subject, such as the individual man or the individual horse." We have restated in a more formal way what is quoted here.

6Words are signs of what is in the mind, and words *taken as spoken sounds* or as *written marks* are not predicated. Predication refers to comparisons of notions or concepts together with their union or separation in the mind. For a more detailed discussion of what predication is see Thomas D. Sullivan, "Between Thoughts and Things: The Status of Meanings," *The New Scholasticism,* Vol. L, 1, winter, 1976.

PART II

THE MULTIPLICITY OF SUBSTANCES

CHAPTER 6

ANCIENT VIEWS OF NATURAL THINGS

A. Theories of one substance

Whether one reads a history of philosophy or a history of science he quickly discovers that the systematic investigation of nature began with Thales of Miletus, a Greek who lived in the sixth century B.C. His aim was to account for the production and destruction of natural things without invoking gods; so whatever merit myths have as metaphorical explanations, Thales realized that systematic accounts are of a different kind. He understood that we have to begin by looking within things for an account of them; we begin with the intrinsic constituents as the explanatory principles to be sought first.

Thales' task was difficult. When we imagine ourselves in his shoes, unequipped with modern instruments, confronting the array of nature with only unaided senses and native wit, we begin to see how inherently arduous investigating the natural world is. And when we think about the years of labor that were necessary to bring modern scientific theories to their development, we ought to pause before we regard ancient accomplishments with disrespect.

Thales, as well as the pre-Socratic investigators who followed him, proposed a theory of materials. He held that natural entities are all made of water and that all differences in their properties are founded upon one primary quality, the relative density of the water in them. Natural production and destruction consisted, he thought, in water becoming thinner or thicker, more rare or more condensed. Stated in contemporary language, natural coming to be and passing away consisted fundamentally in varying the density of the one substance. What today we call changes in state or phase, changes from the solid to the liquid to the gaseous state, seem to be the sort of thing Thales had in mind. Other variations of qualities, those of color, shape, ductility, viscosity, etc., are founded on differences in the density of the one substance or material.

Thales' position becomes more intelligible than it first appears if we take note of some of the observations that lend it support. For instance: boiled water becomes vaporous and less dense. Metals, and sand, too, become liquid under intense heat, which suggests that they have a liquid base. Living things depend upon water and have a large amount of it in them, and of course water is very abundant in nature. In short, Thales thought water was a universal material from which things come to be and into which they pass away through variations in density.

Other pre-Socratics also held theories of one substance. Some posited air as the stuff, some fire, some a material that could not be identified with anything observable. None, however, held what we would call rock--or better, mineral--to be the one substance. These other theories also held that things come to be and pass away through variations in density.

B. Theories of more than one substance

The alternative to one substance is more than one, and a number of the pre-Socratic philosopher-scientists postulated a multiplicity of them. Some proposed two, some three, and some more; but the most enduring theory was first articulated by Empedocles. He claimed that there were four elementary materials: earth, water, air, and fire; and he thought they were combined in varying proportions, as one varies the ingredients of a solution. Indeed, his notion of a mixed body corresponds to our notion of a solution, whether solid, liquid, or gaseous. Combining the elements in many ways according to different proportions produced the many stuffs and things in nature, while separating the elements destroyed the same things or stuffs. Such a view of natural production and destruction was the consequence of proposing a plurality of permanent elements from which everything else comes to be.

Empedocles' theory of four substance-materials accords in fair measure with ordinary, unaided observation. As a modern author says, "air, rock, water, and sunlight--these are the four sources from which come all living things and their environment."[1] The ancient theory was founded on what we know as the gaseous, liquid, and solid states that are the general qualitative conditions under which natural stuffs exist. Fire is on the list of elementary substances because heat is necessary for the life of organisms and for qualitative changes in stuffs. The effects of furnaces on ores underscore the active role of heat in bringing about changes in stuffs. In short, for Empedocles, natural production and destruction were processes of combining and separating, and the specifying property of things was the proportion of the materials constituting them.

Obtaining evidence for a theory of several materials is more difficult than our words so far suggest. In order to show *that* a plurality of stuffs exists, we must observe something decompose into other stuffs that are qualitatively different from the original composite. We must also observe the reverse process, discovering stuffs that can be combined to form something new which is qualitatively different from the original ingredients. Ordinary experience, however, does not provide much evidence; nature does not give us ready illustrations of such combining and separating processes. As they appear to unaided observation, the death and decay of organisms are too indeterminate to support a theory of several materials. Without instruments, dead animals and plants do not clearly show us qualitatively different ingredients, nor do ordinary observations of changes such as the rusting of iron reveal a combining of distinct stuffs. Hence we are hardly surprised to find that a theory of many substances was proposed only after the metallurgical, glass-making, and dye-making arts had been developed.

When one smelts an ore he begins with a stuff which through heating separates a pure metal from a qualitatively different residue. Similarly, the sand, soda ash, limestone, etc., from which primitive glasses appear to have been made, all differ in their properties from the finished product. The same can be said about the production of dyes. Thus, only after man had acquired a certain technology was there evidence to suggest a theory of several substances as a more satisfactory account of natural things. And that is what we ought to expect, for chemically active materials quickly form the stable compounds which make up the familiar natural world. Only when they are acted upon by some agency (such as a furnace) that is more than ordinarily intense do the ingredients separate or combine to form new stuffs.

C. Atomic theories

The theories sketched above dealt with materials that were regarded as continuous; that is, the theories did not proclaim stuffs to be constituted of indivisible units called "atoms." Nevertheless, early in the history of philosophy-science, atomic hypotheses were put forward. Among the early Greeks the principal atomists were Leucippus and Democritus. Later, in the first century B.C., the Roman poet Lucretius wrote a treatise on atomism called *De Rerum Natura* (On the Nature of Things).

Essentially these early atomic theories were alike, for all postulated atoms as the ultimate realities out of which things are made. According to Lucretius, the atoms had different shapes, were in motion, were separated by the void, collided, occupied positions, and were put together in an order. His theory held every entity to be either an atom or an arrangement of atoms, which meant that structure differentiated one macroscopic thing or stuff from another. As a consequence, coming to be and passing away were taken to be processes of combining and separating atoms, but the combining and separating processes were unlike those of Empedocles.

D. The common position: a philosophical summary

Having described the views of three different pre-Socratic theories, we must now examine them to see what they held in common about the distinction and origin of things. First we should note that the theories tacitly assumed that any thing which comes to be, comes to be from an already existing thing; new entities are not produced by nature out of nothing. Second, the theories all maintained that the processes of coming to be and passing away consist in a modification of a property or properties of a permanent substance or substances. In short, all the theories held natural entities to be property-things. Thales held that one substance underwent a kind of thickening and thinning to bring about various kinds of things. Empedocles held that things come to be and pass away through mixing determinate amounts of elementary substances according to proportions or through separating them. The atomists held that individual substance-things combined in determinate numbers according to an order or arrangement. So as we said, the pre-Socratic theories held a common position *insofar as they implicitly conceived macroscopic entities to be property-things*. Because substances were held to be permanent, natural production had to be a modification of a property or properties that brought about distinct *property-things* conceived in the likeness of artefactual entities, which serve as models for our conceptions of natural property-things.

Notes to Chapter 6

[1]John H. Storer, *The Web of Life*, a Signet Book (New York: The New American Library, Inc., 1956), p. 26.

CHAPTER 7

NEWER VIEWS OF NATURAL THINGS

A. The common view

The entities that are most obviously things are organisms, and one could select nearly at random from among textbooks to discover that many biologists hold organisms to be explicable as a set of chemical reactions and physical processes. We read, for instance, that

> the *mechanist* view of life holds that all phenomena, no matter how complex, are ultimately describable in terms of physical and chemical laws and that no "vital force" distinct from matter and energy is required to explain life. . . .Man, then, is a machine-- an enormously complex machine, but a machine, nevertheless.[1]

The authors' position is partly explained by their opposition to vitalism (which is not a lively issue today), and perhaps it ought to be read more as a denial of that position than as an affirmation of mechanism. Mechanism is not, however, confined to authors of

biology texts, for the philosophers who a few years ago supported
the mind-brain identity theory subscribed to a position that comes
to the same thing. D.M. Armstrong, for instance, claimed that one
view

> bids fair to become established scientific doctrine.
> This is the view that can give a complete account of
> man in purely physico-chemical terms.[2]

As Herbert Feigl, a man of similar conviction, puts it, the problem
as it is seen by the proponents of the mind-brain identity theory
consists

> in the challenge to render an adequate account of the
> relation of the 'raw feels', as well as of other mental
> facts (intentions, thoughts, volitions, desires, etc.), to
> the corresponding neurophysiological processes.[3]

And regarding the answer to the problem, Feigl says:

> The solution that appears most plausible to me, and
> that is entirely consistent with a thoroughgoing
> naturalism, is an *identity theory* of the mental and
> the physical as follows: Certain neurophysiological
> terms denote (refer to) the very same events that are
> also denoted (referred to) by certain phenomenal
> terms. The identification of the objects of this twofold
> reference is of course logically contingent, although
> it constitutes a very fundamental scientific outlook . .
> . . we may say that neurophysiological terms and the
> corresponding phenomenal terms, though widely
> differing in sense, and hence in the modes of
> confirmation of statements containing them, do have
> identical *referents*.[4]

Feigl claims that although the terms employed in ordinary speech differ from those of physiological discourse, the referents of each, the realities themselves, are neurophysiological events, which amounts to saying that the referents are no more than chemical and physical processes. Thus, the mind-brain identity theory is mechanistic in its view of organisms, as is behaviorism. The word "mechanist" comes from "machine," to which men and other organisms are likened, and the analogy--metaphor we might better say at this point--has some justification; for both kinds of entities are organized, structured systems, both have heterogeneous parts that affect one another, both utilize energy, etc. In short, there is a similarity between them. But the important point is that organisms are considered to be property-things specified and constituted by an arrangement, a structure; their similarity to machines consists therein.

B. The machine metaphor

The mechanical view is not new. As long ago as several hundred years Thomas Hobbes described human artefacts as artificial animals:

> Nature, the art whereby God hath made and governs the world, is by the *art* of man, as in many other things, so in this also imitated, that it can make an artificial animal. For seeing life is but a motion of limbs, the beginning whereof is in some principal part within; why may we not say, that all *automata* (engines that move themselves by springs and wheels as doth a watch) have an artificial life? For what is the *heart*, but a *spring*; and the *nerves*, but so many *strings*; and the *joints*, but so many *wheels*, giving motion to the whole body, such as was intended by the artificer?[5]

Hobbes is clear: organisms are like machines; in our terms they are property-things.

Descartes, who came later than Hobbes, is more elaborate in his description. The human body, he maintains, is an organization of materials moved by a soul which stands outside the body:

> These [hypothetical] men shall be composed, as we are, of a soul and a body; . . .the body is nothing else than a statue or machine of clay which God forms expressly to make it as nearly like as possible to ourselves, so that not only does he give it externally the colour and the form of all our members, but also he puts within it all the parts necessary to make it walk, eat, breathe and, in fine, imitate all those of our functions which may be supposed to proceed from matter and to depend merely on the arrangement of organs.

> . . . the particles of blood which penetrate to the brain . . . serve not only to nourish and support its substance, but chiefly, also to produce there a certain very subtle breath, or rather flame, very active and very pure, which is called the *animal spirits*. . . .

> . . . the nerves of the machine that I am describing to you may very well be compared to the pipes of the machinery of these [hydraulically operated] fountains, its muscles and its tendons to various other engines and devices which serve to move them, its animal spirits to the water which sets them in motion, of which the heart is the spring, and the cavities of the brain the outlets. . . . And finally, when the *reasonable soul* shall be in this machine, it will have its principal seat in the brain [in the pineal gland], and it will be there *like the fountain-maker* [emphasis mine], who must be at the openings where all the pipes of these machines discharge themselves, if he wishes to start, to stop, or change in any way their movements.

> . . . consider that all these functions follow naturally in this machine simply from the arrangement of its

parts, no more nor less than do the movements of a
clock or other automata, from that of its weights and
its wheels. . . .[6]

Descartes' words are plain as they stand: he views the body as an
arrangement of parts moved by a rational soul which (elsewhere) is
described as an immaterial substance extrinsic to the body just as
the fountain-maker is extrinsic to the pipes he controls. Because
Descartes claims that man has a separate, rational soul which controls his body, Descartes' view is the paradigm of dualism. Though
he is not a mechanist, his position makes the whole man--body and
soul--a property-thing constituted by an arrangement, a structure,
and to that extent his position is the same as the mechanist's.
Although Descartes' man has a spiritual element in him, he is
nonetheless a property-thing.

What began with Hobbes and Descartes has become more
clearly detailed in modern times, for the mechanical analogy
between living and non-living has been strengthened by the
development of modern biology and also by the development of
modern machines, particularly servo-mechanisms which imitate
complex human behavior and which have more sophisticated
functions than the automata of an earlier day. We can find many
accounts which compare organisms to machines; but one, an essay
by William Seifriz, puts the mechanistic position more fundamentally and clearly than most.

After he has pointed out that one might classify machines
according to energy sources or structures, Seifriz settles on the
latter as the proper basis of classification. Structure, he says, is an
arrangement of parts which adequately accounts for the activities
that distinguish the living from the non-living:

The proteins of which protoplasm is made acquire
the property of life through a specific arrangement of
parts into an harmonious whole, somewhat in the
same way that a clock attains the unique quality of
time-keeping through the perfect coordination of its
parts. The wheels of a clock stand in a definite
relationship to one another, and unless so arranged
the clock will not function. Regularity of motion is

the specific quality which has arisen as the result of
perfect coordination. This new property is an
attribute which is not possessed by an individual part
of the clock nor by all parts unless they are
assembled in a specific way. As each wheel of the
clock is put into place, the mechanism increases in
complexity, but the capacity to keep time is not
acquired until the last wheel is in position. The
placing of the last wheel is a no more intricate act
than the placing of any other wheel, yet the moment
it is done, a new property suddenly comes into being.
The acquisition of the capacity to keep time is a
distinct step elevating the clock from a class of
functionless mechanisms to a class of organized
mechanisms possessing the unique quality of time-
keeping. Similarly has non-living matter acquired
life through structural organization. The attainment
of this function is a discrete step and not a gradual
transition; that is to say, the change from the non-
living to the living is not continuous. Life has come
into being suddenly. Such a postulate is no more
vitalistic than that which ascribes the origin of the
function of time-keeping to the placing of a wheel in a
clock.[7]

Seifriz maintains that the appearance of vital activities in an
organism is accomplished by completing the structure. Just as a
clock acquires the new property of time-keeping when the last part
is positioned, so too an organism begins to live when its last part
falls into place.

At this point we ought to emphasize that machines are made of
natural materials that have been acted upon by human art.
Manufacturing processes, whether primitive or sophisticated,
fashion natural materials into artefacts by introducing
determinate dimensions, shapes, and order, all of which are
properties. Hence in comparing organisms to machines, we need
no new philosophic categories or concepts. The "machine" view,
despite differences of detail, does not differ from the philosophic
theory of the ancient philosopher-scientists examined in the
previous chapter. However complex it maybe, an arrangement, a

structure that orders independent parts or particles--whatever their nature--is a relational property of the parts or particles. Put another way, a more complex structure is not different in kind from one that is less complex; it is only more difficult to describe and to comprehend.

In sum, we may say that modern times have come to see the machine taken as an analogue of natural property-things. The analogy is employed for the purpose of defending the view that organisms are the same kind of natural entity as the machine.

C. Counter opinions

Although mechanism is a commonly held position, it is not without opponents. No less a biologist than A.I. Oparin tells us:

> Quite large numbers of scientists now take the view that an understanding of life in general involves no more than a very thorough explanation of all vital phenomena in terms of physical and chemical processes. According to this view there are no specifically biological laws, and the rules which prevail in the inorganic world also govern all the phenomena taking place in living organisms. But this amounts to denying all the essential differences between organisms and the objects of the inorganic world, which is fundamentally unsound. Certainly life is material in nature, but it is not inherent in every form of material. It is a manifestation of a special form of motion which we find only in organisms and which is absent from the objects of the inorganic world. This form of motion of matter, in addition to obeying the general physical and chemical laws, also has its own specific laws. If one is to understand life it is therefore important to take into account these qualitative differences from other forms of motion.[8]

Organisms have their own motions, their own laws; so one cannot justifiably be a mechanist, Oparin says, because mechanism requires him to deny the essential difference between organisms and inanimate entities. His position is clear, and it makes an important point: mechanism has opponents other than the all but disappeared vitalists. But if Oparin subscribes to dialectical materialism (which appears to be the case), his opposition to mechanism cannot be unambiguous. Dialectical materialism holds mental phenomena, for example, to result from a particular organization of matter; and to be understood in a non-mechanistic way, that statement requires an elaboration which dialectical materialism does not provide. To put the issue more determinately, if the organization which gives rise to mental phenomena is a property, then the Marxists place themselves in the same basic category as the mechanists; they make organisms to be property-things, however different they may be in some respects.

The difficulty of the problem which organisms pose becomes more apparent when we consider what another biologist who opposes both mechanism and vitalism has to say:

What position should the biologist take today if he wishes to avoid that dilemma the horns of which are vitalism and mechanism? The most familiar solution of this difficulty is to adopt the position commonly called "organicism," which is simply a recognition of the fact that living stuff has the remarkable organizing capacities which the student of development has demonstrated. This is little more, however, than admission that the problem exists. The organicist is bound, I think, to be agnostic in his biology in that he simply does not know whence this strange organizing power arises. . . . Something there surely is in any living thing which pulls dead, random matter into the form of an organized individual and holds it steadily there through material flux and change. The moment death occurs a radical alteration takes place, for this integrating force is gone and the bodily materials at once begin to break up into randomness again. This organizing

> power is life's peculiar quality. It never seems to
> arise spontaneously but is passed along from one
> organism to its offspring in a kind of apostolic
> succession, without a break.[9]

Organicism rejects both the mechanistic and the vitalistic account; yet as Sinnott concedes, it does not offer a clear alternative. All he is willing to say is that there is *something*, whatever it may be, that organizes chemicals into an organism. Though such a statement can hardly be wrong, and though it does not contribute much to the issue, it is not, we should note, dualistic.

Nobel Laureate Ragnar Granit is of like mind about the inadequacy of physics and chemistry alone to account for organisms:

> One often encounters the implicit notion that the
> ultimate aim of biology must be to explain its
> findings in terms of physics or chemistry. By
> discussing relevant examples, I have tried to show
> that such explanations indeed are important but may
> be so without ever touching fundamental questions
> concerning living organisms in their relation to the
> environment. Impulses, for instance, are alike in all
> sensory nerve fibers and their genesis is reasonably
> well understood in physico-chemical terms, yet this
> knowledge does not help us very much to understand
> their different effects on the senses.[10]

His text needs no comment, except to say that his argument from the similarity of impulses and their different effects will be taken up in a later chapter.

Another opponent of both vitalism and mechanism declares himself very bluntly about the machine theory of organisms:

> In the history of science and philosophy there is
> hardly a less happy expression than that of the bête
> machine of Descartes. No concept leads to such a

distorted view of the problem underlying it or so greatly falsifies its proper meaning. It might even be said that, in spite of its heuristic success, the notion of the machine has had a destructive effect on the development of biological theory. It has entangled the investigator even today with scholastic artificial problems, and at the same time has prevented the clear discernment of the essential problem of organic nature. Only the displacement of the machine theory which is now gradually taking place will put an end to the paralysis of biological thinking for which this Cartesian expression has been responsible.

What makes the machine theory useless is the fact that it is unsuitable for the very purpose for which it was introduced, namely, the physico-chemical analysis of vital processes. . . .[11]

Von Bertalanffy's opposition to the machine theory is so thorough-going that he denies even the value of the analogy that might be developed:

. . .we cannot speak of a machine 'theory' of the organism, but at most of a machine fiction. It can mean nothing to say that an organism 'is' a machine in the sense in which the physicist--without saying anything metaphysical--asserts that bodies 'are' constructed of atoms. We could at most say that organisms can be regarded 'as if' they were machines. We do not at all wish to underestimate the value of picturable fictions in science, but we cannot remain satisfied with the one offered in the present case. If biology is able to offer us no hypothesis for dealing with its most fundamental problem--the organization of materials and processes--but only a doubtful meta-phor, then we can only regard this as a declaration of intellectual bankruptcy. Moreover, even as a fiction the machine idea does not attain its goal, because, as

we have said, it proves to be inadequate in the face of
a large and important section of biological data.[12]

As the reader can see, there is no ambiguity in these statements.
Still, we have not yet considered Von Bertalanffy's more formal
statement of his objection, a statement that actually precedes the
passages we have just cited:

> . . . a simple physico-chemical explanation of the
> single processes leaves us in the lurch in the face of
> the fundamental biological problem--the organiza-
> tion of materials and processes in the organism. In
> order to deal with this we are driven, whether we like
> it or not, to introduce a theory of the structure of
> living things which surpasses the mere physico-
> chemical analysis.[13]

Vitalism and mechanism, he claims, do not account for the
organization of materials and processes in organisms. What we
need is a theory of structure which surpasses a physico-chemical
analysis. Thus he says:

> . . . we postulate a new discipline called *General
> System Theory*. Its subject matter is the formulation
> and derivation of those principles which are valid for
> "systems" in general.[14]

Systems in general are the subject matter of a new discipline, a
kind of philosophy, which aims to provide principles common to all
systems, no matter where they occur or to what science they
belong. Moreover, such a theory is thought necessary (in part)
because

> classical physics. . .was highly successful in develop-
> ing the theory of unorganized complexity. Thus, for

example, the behavior of a gas is the result of the unorganized and individually untraceable movements of innumerable molecules; as a whole it is governed by the laws of thermodynamics. In contrast, the fundamental problem today is that of organized complexity. Concepts like those of organization, wholeness, directiveness, teleology, and differentiation are alien to conventional physics. However, they pop up everywhere in the biological, behavioral and social sciences, and are, in fact, indispensable for dealing with living organisms or social groups.[15]

Then a bit later he tells us more about what he means when he says that systems are wholes and how such wholes affect the study of parts that make them up:

While in the past, science tried to explain observable phenomena by reducing them to an interplay of elementary units investigatable independently of each other, conceptions appear in contemporary science that are concerned with what is somewhat vaguely termed "wholeness," i.e., problems of organization, phenomena not resolvable into local events, dynamic interactions manifest in the difference of behavior of parts when isolated or in a higher configuration, etc.; in short, "systems" of various orders not understandable by investigation of their respective parts in isolation.[16]

General system theory considers organized systems in general and on that account must occupy itself with problems related to wholes and to their parts, the parts not being understandable outside the whole. The point bears emphasis: an organism, the theory says, owes its special properties to the whole; their source lies in it. So although they are brief, these statements do tell us how Von Bertalanffy attempts to treat organisms, which he views as one kind of system. Yet if he regards all organization as the result of relational properties, then despite his view of the wholes as origins of new properties, his basic philosophic position is not different: organisms are property-things. Thus it would seem that all the positions we have so far described, no matter what they are called or what they state, presuppose that all changes are modifications of properties that reside in a substance or substances. But we have not finished.

To an Anglo-American mind it might appear strange to hear it said that all matter is psychical in nature:

> The so called 'matter' composing our body seems to be divided into two different kinds. The functions of a large part of our brain cells correspond to mental processes, whereas this is not the case with all other brain and body cells. The 'matter' which composes the psychophysical cells only consists, however, of compounds and atoms, which are known also in the nonliving state. All material which builds up our brain cells finally derives from the food--first from the nourishment which we receive by the placenta, later from the components of our own blood. Besides, most compounds of our brain cells show a rather rapid turnover. As the chemical and electro-physiological functions of these compounds, ions and elementary particles correspond to psychic processes, it seems to be most easily understandable when we suppose that all matter already has a protopsychic nature. But psychic phenomena like sensations originate only in highly complicated stages of integration in neurones and brains, and they can only be experienced in coherent awareness.[17]

Another paragraph contains a general description of this position.

> This philosophical conception . . . is based on the indubitable reality of the psychic phenomena, as analyzed with the help of logical laws of thinking, which were developed phylogenetically by adaption

to the universal logical laws of the world. At the
same time, the results of science, which are normally
obtained without considering the epistemological
basis, were utilized. This combination led to the
establishment of a panpsychistic and realistic
identism. No contrast between mind and matter
could be accepted, and psychical processes were
identified with physiological processes of the brain.
In such a manner epistemological panpsychism is
combined with the realism of natural science, and a
bridge is built to functional materialism.[18]

The human mind, whether it espouses the position described above
or some other, often finds it difficult to believe that anything of any
nature whatever, either stuffs or properties, can actually come into
existence. Nothing really comes to be; only appearances change,
and an appearance is taken to be a manifestation of what is already
present but hidden. That seems to be what Rensch maintains.
This view, which he calls a "panpsychistic identism," is in his mind
a realistic (not idealistic) panpsychism. It postulates that matter
has a "protopsychical" nature, that "mind," if we may call it that, is
inseparable from the fundamental realities of even inanimate
nature. Conscious mental processes become manifest when an
appropriate integration--an order or arrangement--is introduced
into compounds and elementary particles. For Rensch life is indeed
real, so real that he makes all existing things essentially living.
Yet because psychic phenomena--sensations and higher mental
activities--become apparent and show themselves only when
properly integrated, Rensch's position, too, makes organisms to be
arrangements of particles. So although mechanists and pan-
psychists (or animists) assign different characteristics to the
elementary substances, they are basically alike in a fundamental
way. For both, organisms result from a structure imposed upon the
elementary particles. Once again, then, we are confronted with a
theory of natural entities as property-things. (We might note that
Rensch agrees with the mind-brain identity people in making
psychic processes to be physiological. He differs from them in
admitting the reality of the mental and assigning psychic
properties to all matter, a state of affairs that would horrify Feigl
or Armstrong.) There now remains only one point to be made.

As it is expressed by Albert Einstein, the modern scientific position actually embraces the philosophical views of Thales and Empedocles, dressed in modern garb, of course. In one of his books Einstein tells us:

> We have two realities: *matter and field* . . . . From the relativity theory we know that matter represents vast stores of energy and that energy represents matter. We cannot, in this way, distinguish qualitatively between matter and field, since the distinction between mass and energy is not a qualitative one. By far the greatest part of energy is concentrated in matter; but the field surrounding the particle also represents energy, though in an incomparably smaller quantity. We could therefore say: Matter is where the concentration of energy is great, field is where the concentration of energy is small. But if this is the case, then the difference between matter and field is a quantitative rather than a qualitative one.[19]

Matter and field: they are both energy, and they differ only in their concentration, their density, their "thinness" or "thickness," how rare or condensed they are. So if energy is the one stuff out of which everything is made, then at root all coming to be must be a variation in concentration, in the density of the one elementary stuff. In that case arranging particles in combinations has to be a secondary coming to be. Only after energy is converted to particles can we get the kind of structure which atoms, molecules, etc., are thought to require.

Another physicist, Werner Heisenberg, makes the same point in even clearer terms:

> Besides the three fundamental building stones of matter--electron, proton, and neutron--new elementary particles have been found which can be created in these processes of highest energies and disappear again after a short time. The new particles have

similar properties as the old ones except for their stability. Even the most stable ones have lifetimes of roughly only a millionth part of a second, and the lifetimes of others are even a thousand times smaller. At the present time about twenty-five different new elementary particles are known; the most recent one is the negative proton.

These results seem at first sight to lead away from the idea of the unity of matter, since the number of fundamental units of matter seems to have again increased to values comparable to the number of different chemical elements. But this would not be a proper interpretation. The experiments have at the same time shown that the particles can be created from other particles. Actually the experiments have shown the complete mutability of matter. All the elementary particles can, at sufficiently high energies, be transmuted into other particles, or they can be created from kinetic energy and can be annihilated into energy, for instance into radiation. Therefore, we have here actually the final proof for the unity of matter. All the elementary particles are made of the same substance, which we may call energy or universal matter; they are just forms in which matter can appear.[20]

Heisenberg is clear: all things in nature come from one fundamental substance, which as Einstein said earlier, varies according to concentration. If one holds that there is one substance in nature, he can have no other view of the production of things. So it would seem that as far as common philosophical conceptions are concerned, those conceptions that arise from common experience, there is nothing new under the sun.

D. Essentials of the main positions recapitulated

The modern positions described in the foregoing all consider organisms to be property-things, but the positions vary in the kinds of property-things they postulate.

1. The mechanist adopts the view that organisms are arrangements of atoms and molecules wholly explicable by physics and chemistry. The machine serves as an analogue in the light of which organisms are to be considered.
2. Descartes makes man a property-thing, one part of which is a rational soul, the other a body of organized physical substances. Man is a dualistic property-thing. (Animals and plants, however, are not dualistic.)
3. Dialectical materialism denies mechanism but makes mental phenomena result from an arrangement; hence entities are property-things.
4. General Systems Theory grounds the special properties of organisms in the whole; but the whole is a property-thing.
5. Rensch makes all matter psychical, but he too considers organisms to be property-things.
6. Some physicists maintain that the conversion of radiation to particles, and particles to radiation, is a variation of density (concentration). The formation of entities through arrangements of particles is then a secondary coming-to-be.

Notes to Chapter 7

[1]Arthur J. Vander, James H. Sherman, Dorothy S. Luciano, *Human Physiology* (New York: McGraw-Hill, Inc., 1970), p. 1.

[2]"The Nature of Mind," in *Mind-Brain Identity Theory*, ed. Clive Vernon Borst (New York: St. Martin's Press, 1970), p. 67.

[3]"Mind-body, not a Pseudo-Problem," *Mind-Brain Identity Theory*, p. 35.

[4]Ibid., p. 38.

[5]*Leviathan*, Collier Books (New York: The Crowell-Collier Publishing Company, 1962), p. 19.

[6]"Selections from the Treatise on Man," in *Descartes Selections*, ed. Ralph M. Eaton (New York: Charles Scribner's Sons), pp. 350-54.

[7]"A Materialistic Interpretation of Life," in *Philosophy of Science* (1939), VI, pp. 266-84.

[8]*The Origin of Life on the Earth*, trans. Ann Synge (New York: Academic Press, Inc., 1957), p. 347.

[9]Edmund W. Sinnott, *The Biology of the Spirit* (London: Victor Gollancz Ltd., 1956), pp. 108-9.

[10]*The Purposive Brain* (Cambridge, Massachusetts: MIT Press, 1977), p. 21.

[11]Ludwig Von Bertalanffy, *Modern Theories of Development*, Harper Torchbooks (New York: Harper & Brothers, 1962), p. 36.

[12]Ibid., p. 38.

[13]Ibid., p. 36.

[14]*General System Theory* (New York: George Braziller, 1968), p. 32.

[15]Ibid., p. 34.

[16]Ibid., pp. 36-7.

[17]Bernhard Rensch, "Polynomistic Determination of Biological Processes," in *Studies in the Philosophy of Biology*, ed. Francisco José Avala and Theodosius Dobzhansky (Berkeley and Los Angeles: University of California Press, 1974), p. 250.

[18]Bernhard Rensch, "Evolution of Matter and Consciousness and its Relation to Panpsychistic Identism," in *Essays in Evolution and Genetics in Honor of Theodosius Dobzhansky* (New York: Appleton-Century-Crofts, 1970), p. 117.

[19]Albert Einstein and Leopold Infeld, *The Evolution of Physics* (New York: Simon and Schuster, 1954), pp. 256-7.

[20]*Physics and Philosophy*, World Perspective Series (New York: Harper and Brothers, 1958), pp. 70-71.

CHAPTER 8

THE ARTEFACTUAL AS PARADIGM

A. Introduction

Philosophers tend to illustrate what they say by using artefacts as examples, which seems reasonable. Men understand rather well the purposes, functions, designs, and materials of artefacts, and that makes them able to throw light on the works of nature, which are more obscure. In other words, because we cause artefacts, they are more intelligible to us than the works of nature; so following our instinctive inclinations, we use the things we make as models to illumine natural entities. On that account we shall have to examine the artefactual to see whether and to what extent it might reveal the character of the natural.

B. The need for artefacts

Quite apart from anthropologists, philosophers as diverse as Aristotle and Frederick Engels have commented on man's need to be a tool-making and tool-using animal. We have to make and use these things to supply for our species "deficiency," and that is the point we shall consider first.

Animals other than man act upon the objects in their environment directly. They attack prey with claws, horns, or other bodily parts, and they escape by the same means. Animals feed directly on carcasses or plants by using their mouths, beaks, or other appendages, and they build houses, nests, and dens by means of the same parts. Their physical features also proportion animals to the climate of their habitat, for their hair, fur, feathers, scales, etc., enable them to adjust to temperature, rain, snow, and other weather conditions. In comparison, man might appear deficient because he is born "organically naked," having neither fur nor feathers nor scales, etc. He comes unequipped with claws, tusks, antlers, or horns and is not swift to escape. In short, man's appendages and parts by themselves do not proportion him to his environment.

But despite this "deficient" human condition, few men would opt for the alternatives of other species. Man prefers his privations to their bounty, for man's intelligence gives him a universal adaptability that enables him to live nearly anywhere, though he prefers some habitats to others. But to serve his intelligence, he requires a universal instrument that equips him to make and to employ tools and utensils; namely, he needs his hand. The human hand[1] is too generalized to be well suited to specific tasks such as preparing foods, eating, drinking, providing clothing and shelter, and the like; yet it is well suited to making and using knives, forks, spoons, and other utensils. Thus, the general purpose of simple tools and utensils is to *proportion* man to his environment, and in their basic character they are extensions of man and subordinate to his needs.

C. Function and structure in artefacts

Artefacts are made for their functions, which in turn account for artefactual structures or forms. For instance, at some time in the past someone wanted to divide a log into parts so that he could handle it more easily, and being inventive he conceived a blade with teeth to be suitable for the job, thereby designing the saw. The structure of the saw is a shape imposed upon suitable materials, which become a blade fitted with a handle. Generally, simple tools and utensils consist of one part invested with a function and another part that can be grasped and moved by the hand. More complicated tools have more than one function and more than two distinguishable parts. In all, however, their special property as artefacts is their human utility; their whole nature is to be an extension of human operations.

It is not hard to see what we do to produce artefacts. Starting with natural materials, we impose on them at most three properties: (1) determinate dimensions, (2) shapes, and (3) a spatial order. Human activities introduce only those properties into the materials, whether the artefact is physically useful or, as in the case of a painting or statue, cognitively useful. Those are the limits, generically viewed, of human causality in relation to artefacts;[2] the human utility that is their generic property results from these three properties, and it is in a real sense "new" or "emergent."

D. Machines

The human activities that produce machines are like those that produce tools insofar as they introduce determinate dimensions, shapes, and structures into materials. And although every such structure presupposes both shapes and dimensions, it establishes a machine's nature by ordering the parts in view of the function. But machines differ from tools, even though a line dividing the two classes cannot be drawn with exactitude. Unlike tools and utensils, machines are ordinarily powered by sources of energy other than human beings (let us exclude animals also), the earliest sources having been the spontaneous movements of wind and water. Modern machines are usually driven by electric, diesel, gasoline, or steam engines; and the energy source is the principal difference between utensils and tools on the one hand and machines on the other. Of course some things we classify as tools are powered by small motors, yet even these require human activity for their application and control. However, the distinction between tools and machines need not be perfectly precise, since the imprecision does not prevent our seeing the chief characteristic of machines.

E. The machine as a medium

If someone wishes to make a pot of tea, he puts a kettle on the stove and allows it to heat. Here a human agent applies a generalized natural agent, a flame, to a specialized, determinate recipient, the water contained in the teakettle, to produce an effect; and though the action is simple, it shows the basic operational character of machines.

Clocks are familiar, so they have often been used as paradigms or models for organisms. Their behavior consists in the regular rotation of two hands on a shaft brought about by a spring distorted through winding. Because the spring is elastic it spontaneously tends to return to its original configuration, and since the restorative movement can be impeded, we are able to apply the spring to gears that successively move one another, rotating the hands in a regular way. The rotation of the hands is produced by directing the movement of the spring through what is called a "causal chain," which means that the mechanism between the spring and hands is a *medium* for applying the spring in a controlled way. In its essentials the rotation is like the heating of the kettle, for in both cases human agents apply general natural agencies to produce controlled, restricted changes that men find useful. The difference is that whereas heating the water requires no "in-between" mechanism, the rotation of the hands cannot occur without it. The mechanism also renders the change or modification regular. But most importantly, the nature of a machine as a medium and as *an instrument* shows that a machine presupposes both the active power that is applied and a passive capacity that is affected. From this point of view, therefore, *machines originate nothing*.

Automobiles provide another, albeit more complex, example. In them a carburetor (or some injection device) introduces an air-gasoline mixture into a chamber where, after ignition, the mixture reacts to form new products that spontaneously expand. The spontaneous motion of the expanding gases is directed upon a piston which moves a crankshaft, which in turn moves a driveshaft, etc., until finally the wheels rotate. Here, too, we have a causal chain that produces a regular movement. In sum, then, when we look at machines from the point of view of their activities, we see that they apply already existing natural agencies to move artefactually shaped and quantified materials already possessing a capacity to be affected. And though most machines are more remote from human life than tools and utensils, they too are extensions of man; they are instruments useful for human activities.

To repeat a central point: machines are media for putting a kettle on the stove; that is, machines are devices that allow us to direct in a regular way the application of a spontaneous energy source to bring about a determinate movement or modification that would not occur otherwise. Let us make no mistake. Heating is an effect of an already existing natural agency. *Considered in its kind*, heating, whether of a kettle by the stove or the sea by the sun, is a natural effect of a natural power. But *directing* the heat of the stove to a kettle is the consequence of human causality. The same is true when the elastic spring rotates a shaft and when expanding gases move a piston. In every one of these cases an existing natural agency is directed and applied by human actions in a way not open to nature upon an object that is able to be affected by the agency; it does no more. As a consequence of the structure of the parts, the effect of the natural agent is limited and moderated in a way that proves useful to men.

The kettle and the stove show something else. No one would claim that putting the kettle on the stove makes the two things one entity per se. The cause-effect relation between them does not of itself bring that about, and even were we to bolt the kettle to the stove, we still would not have one entity per se. Instead we would have two entities that are incidentally one insofar as a mechanical link prohibits one from changing its location without the other moving too.

In the same way, machines are not one entity per se but many that are joined to make an incidental unit, an entity *per accidens*. The sensory impression given by a machine that is enclosed in a housing, or that is locally moveable only as a unit by reason of its linkages, must not cloud the issue, for a machine is no more an entity per se than the kettle and the stove.

Earlier we saw that William Seifriz claimed that clocks have a "new property," that of time keeping; but we should note that "time keeping" is equivocal. It can mean the regular motion of the clock, or the mental activity in us by which we measure the duration of something by using a clock; and the regular movement of the hands is for the sake of the comparative or measuring activity of the mind. There is not, then, a genuinely new kind of movement or behavior in a machine; a directed, restricted application to an existing, general agency does not bring about an effect that is new in kind. So if machines are models for natural things, if the view of natural entities as property-things is right, then we shall expect to find new applications of old agencies; that is, entities such as organisms will apply generalized inanimate forces through their structures to bring about restricted effects one in kind with those of inanimate nature. And such natural entities will be incidental units.

F. Aggregates

Now that we have completed our consideration of artefacts, we must fill out a little the notion of *property-thing* by way of describing certain aggregates and wholes; for aggregates are the property-things offered as paradigms for natural entities. Moreover, the term "property-thing" is awkward, whereas "aggregate" is acceptable, and the thing it names is understood to be constituted by a property.

According to many current views, organisms are arrangements of particles. Lucretius, although he is not a modern figure, held that every macroscopic entity is composed of atoms arranged in a determinate order; and despite the antiquity of its formulator, this statement represents the essential position of every mechanistic theory, whether ancient or modern. Such property-things are usually called "aggregates," and because there is more than one kind, we shall need some distinctions.

We call a collection of marbles an "aggregate." It is a multitude gathered together to form one heap, but other than its quantity it has no distinguishing property. The positions of the marbles in the aggregate make no qualitative difference to the whole, for the marbles are homogeneous and interchangeable with one another. There are, however, other aggregates that are heterogeneous, and they make up the class into which many natural entities are thought to fall, organisms among them. In a heterogeneous aggregate that is not a random mixture the positions of the qualitatively different parts do affect the whole; one cannot be interchanged with another; hence such aggregates are ordered in a determinate way. An army or a football team, for instance, has an order that is founded on functions that depend on skills. Machines have an order based on functions that demand certain shapes and sizes of the parts. So although a homogeneous aggregate does have a spatial order among its parts, the order is not like that of a heterogeneous aggregate. On that account the term "ordered aggregate" will here be used coextensively with "heterogeneous aggregate."

G. Aggregates as wholes

To speak of aggregates as having parts is to imply that they are wholes. Even homogeneous aggregates are quantitative wholes, and of them we like to say, "The whole is equal to the sum of its parts." Ordinarily adding one part to or removing it from such a whole would not cause us to consider the whole as incomplete or defective; rather, the addition or removal would change the count of the aggregate and give us a different whole. On the other hand, aggregates that have differentiated and ordered parts--machines, for instance--are not merely quantitative sums. If they lack a part, they are incomplete or defective and so are not wholes at all. And for this we have already given the reason: ordered aggregates are integrated units the parts of which are proportioned to one another and positioned in relation to one another on the basis of their roles in the whole.

We ought to emphasize that "whole" is a word we attach to observed realities. It signifies something real, not something we arbitrarily construct in our minds. Choosing to consider, say, a patch of blue sky along with Grand Central Station and calling the two a "whole" is not sufficient to make them one. The two "parts" do not have even quantitative unity in reality, much less do they possess an integration founded on function and a proportion of one to the other. Furthermore, even though an incidental collection made up of a beer bottle, a tree stump, a dead cat, and a rusty bucket has a total mass and volume that results from the addition of the amounts of stuff, the collection itself does not otherwise constitute a whole. Thus, "whole" is a word that, like others, is attached to realities on the basis of empirical criteria and is not to be arbitrarily imposed upon collections that are purely mental; only ambiguity and confusion result from such a practice.

And we must stress that the mind, without realizing what it does, often takes the common use of a word to indicate that an identical notion is signified; that is, that the word signifies the same definition in every instance to which it is applied. The medieval Aristotelians called this sort of word--one that signifies many things according to one definition--a "univocal name," whereas a word that signifies many things according to several definitions was said to be an "equivocal name." In many cases the multiple definitions or meanings are obvious because unrelated, as with "pen," which signifies both an enclosure and a writing instrument. But in other cases words have a number of definitions that are related because the realities signified secondarily are related to the one signified primarily as effect to cause, cause to effect, sign to signified, etc., as in Aristotle's famous example of health, which primarily signifies the state of an animal's body, and secondarily a causal relation in food when it it said to be healthy, a sign relation in urine when it is said to be healthy, etc. Words can also have a number of definitions that are related because an extension is made to something secondary that is distinct in kind but similar to that which is primarily signified, as when "father" is first said of a human parent and then extended to politicians who are called city "fathers." In short, a failure to recognize equivocations of this sort can make an adequate definition impossible to obtain.

H. Essential points recapitulated

We may state our main points as follows: (1) the structure of a machine is a spatial ordering of parts; (2) the order is a relation or set of relations; (3) the structure does not bring about modifications in the physical properties of the things that are related; (4) the structure does not bring about a new kind of energy or active power; (5) the regularity of machine behavior is extrinsically caused; (6) machines are not entities per se; they are not one thing per se but only incidentally.

Before we end this chapter let us emphasize the fundamental points contained in(3) and (4). Whether a horse is behind, in front of, or detached from a cart, its properties are the same. Similarly, whether spark plugs are in or out of an engine block, they have the same properties, as do the springs and shafts and gears in or out of a clock; and so it is with every other artefact.

Let us repeat that henceforth when we speak of property-things we shall ordinarily use the term "aggregate" or "ordered aggregate" because that is the sort of property-thing that is at issue in nature; if natural entities are property-things that is the kind they are. It must be noted, however, that occasionally, in the arguments to come in later chapters, the more general word "property-thing" may well be substituted for "aggregate."

Notes to Chapter 8

[1]"Hands" of other animals are not the same as man's, which have thumbs that fully oppose four fingers, a sign of which is that all four limbs of other animals are used for locomotion.

[2]The role of human causality in artificial materials, medicine, and agriculture, as well as other things, will be treated later. But the causality is, we may say, of a different kind.

CHAPTER 9

PHYSICAL PROPERTIES

A. Introduction

The stuffs of inanimate nature are distinguished and defined through their physical properties; and since mechanists claim that organisms are systems of materials unendowed with genuinely new characteristics, it will be useful to have an overview of physical properties so that we can adequately consider whether compounds and organisms are aggregates. No other grounds will suffice for a truly empirical consideration.

B. Solid, liquid, gas

Perhaps the most fundamental physical properties are the solid and fluid states. A fluid can be either liquid or gaseous, so these states provide our most general classification of stuffs: solids, liquids, and gases. Two of the three states manifest characteristic movements. As wind, air spontaneously "blows"; gases of many sorts diffuse through one another, and if they come into existence in empty space, they fill it up. Liquids "flow," and they undergo a motion that is similar to the diffusion of gases; for miscible liquids will disperse through one another. Moreover, if one part of a gas or liquid is heated, a convection current occurs that results from the relative change in density brought about by the heating, a phenomenon that plays a role in producing ocean currents as well as winds. But when we compare fluids to solids we discover that the latter do not have the mobility characteristic of liquids and gases; if they did, they would not be solids. Of course all kinds of stuffs are affected by gravity and, under its influence, fluids that do not chemically react tend to arrange themselves according to their relative density, the more dense toward or in the center of the mass, the less dense farther removed from it. The arrangement of the core, mantle, and crust of the earth is an effect of such an ordering, as is the separation of cream from milk in a bottle. In short, inanimate stuffs can assume an order that has gravity and density as its principles. But now we must turn to other matters.

The descriptions of physical properties that follow correspond to ordinary observations, and in the main the properties will be called by ordinary terms. No attempt will be made here to present them in some particular order, except that hot and cold have been left to the last, for reasons that will appear when they are discussed.

C. Physical properties

Density and weight. Stuffs are more or less dense, and when they are solids we speak of them as being heavier or lighter according to our experience in lifting them.

Shape or form. Every piece of solid stuff has some shape, but many solid stuffs are constituted of small particles that have a distinct crystalline form or shape of a regular geometrical pattern. Minerals, for example, exhibit such forms, six in number. Geologists speak of an "external form" or a "crystalline form" that macroscopic quantities manifest; they also speak of an "internal form" or a "crystalline structure" that is an order of atomic or molecular parts. The internal form or crystalline structure is not observable; it is hypothesized in the theory.

Hardness and softness. Hardness enables a body to resist indentation or cutting or pressure or scratching, etc. Hard bodies are not easily penetrated; their shapes are not easily changed by pressures. Softness is the opposite quality; soft bodies are more easily penetrated, and their shapes are more easily modified. Pliability and plasticity are related to hardness, for pliable bodies are easily shaped by exterior pressing forces, whereas hard bodies are not.

Rigidity and flexibility. Rigid bodies do not easily change their configuration under the influence of external forces; that is, they do not bend easily. Flexible bodies, on the other hand, do bend easily and change their configuration readily.

Breakableness. Stuffs that are able to be separated into parts by being struck are said to be breakable. Not all stuffs break in the same way, and so there are several kinds of breakableness. Some stuffs break into pieces of irregular shape and size. Others break along smooth planes, and geologists say that they *cleave.* A stuff that is breakable is sometimes described as brittle; a stuff that breaks easily is said to be *fragile.* Stuffs that do not break except under very great stress are said to be *unbreakable.*

Malleability. Stuffs that are malleable are able to be shaped by beating or by pressure of some kind.

Ductility. Stuffs that are ductile are able to be bent without breaking; they retain the shape imposed upon them by the bending.

Elasticity. Stuffs that are able to be bent or distorted by a stress and then return to their original configuration are said to be elastic.

Sectility. Stuffs that are able to be cut smoothly are said to be sectile.

Conductivity (thermal). Stuffs that are easily heated by contact are said to be thermally conductive. Stuffs that are not easily heated, which undergo a much slower rise in temperature when exposed to the same source of heat, are said to be *insulative.* The ability to be heated that is described here is an ability that depends upon the contact of the heating source with the heated body; a conductive stuff passes heat along from one of its parts to another.

Conductivity (electrical). Stuffs that are able to be electrified easily are said to be electrically conductive. They offer little resistance to the flow of electric charge. Some gases and liquids are conductive, of course. Stuffs that are not conductive are not able to be electrified except with great difficulty. They offer resistance to the flow of electric charge and are said to be *insulative.*

Magnetism. Stuffs that are able to be magnetized are said to be magnetic. After they become magnetic they can affect other bodies (we are speaking of ferromagnetism).

Color. Stuffs that are colored are able to be seen; they are visible as a consequence of being acted on by a light, that is, by a luminescent body. *Luminescence* enables a body to be seen without an extrinsic aid; such a body is visible by itself. *Luster* is related to color, as is *iridescense.* *Streak* is the geologist's name for the true color of a mineral.

Diaphaneity. Diaphanous stuffs can be penetrated by light; they are *translucent* or *transparent.* Bodies or stuffs that do not transmit light are *opaque.*

Sound, odor, flavor, wetness and dryness. These properties, like color, are related to the sensory organs. Wetness is a property associated with many fluids. Dryness is more commonly associated with gases and solids.

Hotness and coldness. All the properties described above enable a body to *undergo* something; they allow a body to be affected in some way by an extrinsic agency and so are passive; they *do not* enable the body to bring about some modification. On the other hand, hot and cold are properties *by which things affect something else.* A hot body is obviously active; it can modify the temperature of another body and as a consequence can modify its other properties too. Of course, a cold body is considered passive in relation to a hot one, but both are compared to others as active. Stated another way, the property of being hot or cold does not enable a body to *undergo* some modification by an outside agent but rather enables it to heat or cool others.

D. Activity and passivity

Now that we have finished our general descriptions of physical properties we must focus more directly on activity and passivity, so once again we wish to draw attention to the hot and cold as active. Clearly heat is a universal agency in nature for, as we noted above, through it other physical properties are altered. For instance, heating can cause iron to change color, become less electrically conductive, lose its magnetism, ductility, or malleability, and even become liquid and luminescent. Cooling, on the other hand, can restore these properties.

But there is another active characteristic worthy of note that ordinary experience makes especially manifest in liquids, namely, the property of being a solvent. Liquids dissolve solids, other liquids, and gases, thereby facilitating many chemical reactions; for the latter take place most readily in solutions. Moreover, the natural mobility of liquids allows for the widespread distribution of dissolved and suspended stuffs, the most important illustrations of which are the dispersion of minerals, oxygen, and other materials in rivers and seas. Without such dispersion organisms would be extremely handicapped. In sum, there are stuffs which have the property of being a solvent, and in that respect they are active.

The gaseous atmosphere has a similar function, for it transports (evaporated) water and other stuffs (liquids, solids, gases) dissolved or suspended in it; and it distributes oxygen, nitrogen, and carbon dioxide over the planet. However, the dissolving and transporting activity of fluids is secondary to heating and cooling, since it depends on the latter to the extent that the liquid and gaseous states depend on temperature.

Light, as distinct from heat, is also active, especially by making objects visible to organisms endowed with sight.

At this point it is important to note that physical action or activity requires a "system"; that is, physical activity cannot take place unless at least two bodies exist. If the sun were the only body in the universe, no heating action would occur; the sun would be hot, but not heating. In order that the latter exist, there must be something else being heated. The same is true of other physical activities: if there is illumining, there is something being illumined; if there is attracting, there is something being attracted, etc. Thus, no modification of physical qualities occurs outside a system consisting of one body that is the source of the action and another body that undergoes the modification at the hands of the active body; all physical changes require a system.

In summary, let us note that whenever the physical properties of a stuff undergo modification we say that the stuff has undergone a "physical change," and physical changes are passive "undergoings" that require active qualities in extrinsic things to bring them about; that correlation we regularly observe. (Local motion is also a physical change, of course.) The other kind of change that occurs in the inanimate realm is "chemical change," and to that we must pay special attention.

CHAPTER 10

WHETHER COMPOUNDS ARE AGGREGATES

A. Introduction

When we initially posed our problem in Chapter 1 we noted that chemists speak of chemical changes as changes of substance. But if mechanism is right, then every stuff is an aggregate of particles and none is a substance. If atoms are arrangements of particles, then they are aggregates; and if molecules are arrangements of atoms, they too are aggregates. Nothing other than truly elementary particles would be substances. So the issue must be faced.

B. Elements and compounds

When chemical elements are brought together under suitable conditions they undergo a reaction that brings about a compound. The term "reaction" suggests that each element acts on the other, and so it would appear. Reactions also occur when a compound breaks down into constituent elements; so we see that they can be either productive or destructive processes. For our present purposes we need consider only those which produce compounds, for what we say of production will hold for destruction as well. As an example we shall use the coming to be of common salt, sodium chloride, because it is familiar to everyone.

We all know that salt is made from sodium and chlorine, and we also know that sodium and chlorine are described and identified by their physical properties. Sodium is a solid metallic element, one of the alkalai metals; it has a cubic crystalline form, is silvery white in color, soft, malleable, ductile, opaque, electrically and thermally conductive, a little less dense than water, etc. And if some stuff has the entire set of physical properties (not all have been listed), it is sodium, and if it is sodium, then it has the entire set of properties. Chlorine is a gaseous non-metallic element, yellow-green in color, possessed of a disagreeable odor, is denser than air, non-conducting, etc. As with sodium, if a stuff has the entire set of physical properties (not all have been listed) it is chlorine, and if it is chlorine, then it has the set of properties. But when we examine salt, we see we must describe it differently than both the elements. Salt is a solid compound; it has cubic crystals, is breakable, non-conducting, white in color, opaque, possessed of a distinct flavor bearing its own name, etc. Once again, the stuff and its set of descriptive properties are convertible.

Having noted the distinct sets of properties in the elements and the compound, we now must ask a question: is the compound an aggregate or not? And since atomic theory seems to suggest that compounds are indeed aggregates, we must consider some things the theory says.

Atoms are thought to contain two principal parts, a nucleus and an electron cloud. The electron cloud is said to consist of electrons, tiny particles with unit negative charge, located at varying distances from the nucleus. Electrons are difficult to locate, to say the least, but their energy levels can be correlated with the most probable distances from the nucleus, and these energy levels are often called "shells." Electrons are characterized by the specific energy levels (amounts of energy) they have; and it appears that the largest number of shells any atom actually has is seven, although in principle the current theory would allow for more.

The shells themselves can be divided into subshells and the subshells into orbitals, and each of the subdivisions represents a slightly different energy level. They do not, however, represent differences as great as those which separate the shells themselves. The bonding of atoms to one another is thought to be effected by the outermost shells of the combining atoms, which are called "valence shells," and they are stable (the element does not ordinarily react) if they have eight electrons. But if a valence shell has either seven or six electrons, the atom tends to take on one or two more, whereas if it has one, two, or three in its valence shell, it tends to lose them. But whether an atom loses as many as three or gains as many as two electrons, the bonds that are formed through the gain or loss are called "ionic." Atoms that gain or lose electrons are called "ions" by reason of the net negative or positive charge they acquire. Compounds formed by such atoms ionize in solution, and they are said to be electrolytes.

In contrast, an atom with four or five electrons in its valence shell tends to form bonds not by losing or gaining electrons but by "sharing" them in what is called a "covalent" bond. Compounds formed by these atoms do not ionize in solution, and they are said to be non-electrolytes.

Although the description above is rough and limited, it suffices for the point we wish to make: the outermost shell of electrons is thought to account for atomic union and separation; and the theoretical description of the bonding (either ionic or covalent) by means of electrons located in the valence shell portrays the union as establishing an order between two or more atoms which are spatially extrinsic to one another. In other words, *if we limit our considerations to the sort of thing just described*, then a molecule would seem to be an ordered aggregate; it would be a whole constituted as such by a property. And if this kind of description is taken to say all that is relevant to the reaction, then it follows that *the molecule could not have any new physical properties*; it could have no properties that do not already belong to the parts of the aggregate. Let us repeat: if we consider atoms to be only arrangements of preconstituted parts bound together at the periphery by their charges, then their order is the property that gives them unity, and they are therefore property-things. But as we have already noted, an order does not cause already existing properties in a stuff to be destroyed, nor does it cause new kinds of properties to come to be; that is the consequence of the machine view.

The difficulties we encounter when we compare these conceptions to the data are patent. The set of physical properties that describes salt is different from that of sodium and from that of chlorine, and consequently we must say that neither sodium nor chlorine exists *as such* in salt. If either or both did so exist, their characteristic properties would be present. Let us repeat: because observation shows that a new set of properties actually is present in the reaction product, salt cannot be an aggregate, which means that our only remaining alternative is to say that the elements and the compounds that came from them are different substances. But now what are we to say about our theoretical models? Do they without addition explain chemical changes once we maintain that the reaction products are different substances?

If molecules are viewed in the likeness of the machine analogy, then a chemical reaction consists in each atom acting on the other by reason of an active property each already possesses, and each atom undergoing the action of the other by reason of a passive quality each already possesses. And just as the linked parts of a machine do not change their sets of properties, neither would atoms. Such are the implications of a theory that makes compounds to be aggregates.

Reflecting on the theory, we see that the representation of atoms as aggregates *does* account for the union and separation of atoms, but that it *does not* explain the disappearance of some properties and the coming to be of others, except for adding the mass (mass-energy), which is conserved. (We might add that total charge is conserved too.) So given that changes have occurred in almost all the properties, we know that something more than a mere uniting must occur, even though the nature of the additional activities or interactions is left in the dark. That some sort of interaction must occur cannot be doubted, if observation is to mean anything, but *precisely what the character of the interaction is we have no way of determining. Mutatis mutandis,* we are faced with having to say as did Newton when he claimed not to know the nature of gravity: "Hypotheses non fingo." He referred, of course, to assumptions about the what-it-is of gravity. Here the "hypotheses" we wisely forego making (we could never confirm them) are those that would attempt to reveal the nature of the interactions that bring about the appearance and disappearance of properties in elements and compounds. So in summary, though we cannot say *how* a new substance comes to be in a chemical reaction, we are nonetheless obliged to conclude *that* it does.

It is important to emphasize that aggregates which imitate machines do not undergo interactions of the sort that occur among the elements of a compound; they do not undergo interactions that modify the physical properties of their parts. We ought to emphasize the point because we must not inadvertently mix cases.

Every aggregate, it is true, comes to be by combining preexisting entities or stuffs, but we cannot convert the proposition to say that everything that comes to be by combining preexisting substances is an aggregate, for "combining" is an equivocal word. Combining sometimes does make interactions possible, as is plain in chemical reactions. And we also know that an atomic nucleus cannot be merely an aggregate of protons and neutrons; if it were, atoms could not have properties (except for mass and charge) other than those of the nuclear particles; they would be sub-microscopic "piles of marbles." Hence, when nuclear particles come together to bring about atoms they must interact in a way that is analogous to the interaction of chemical elements.

We should note too that chemists produce plastics and other materials not found in nature. Now the sets of conditions as well as the combinations of ingredients which make the reactions possible are artefactually brought about; both the conditions and order of combining are supplied by human causes. This does not mean, however, that the product is an aggregate.

Variations of properties occur as the result of changes of state as, when we expose some stuff to a strong source of heat, the stuff--iron, say--can change its physical state from a solid to a liquid and ultimately to a gas. But such changes are held not to result in a new kind of stuff, even though the liquid and gaseous states are accompanied by a different set of properties. A metal such as iron soon becomes red and luminescent and finally liquifies, at which time it is no longer ductile, elastic, etc. In short, changes of state are usually the result of heating, and changes of state are accompanied by changes in other properties.

If we have a machine that employs heat as an energy source, the latter might get out of control and as a consequence some part could become hot enough to make the machine break down. That is why many need cooling systems; determinate machines presuppose determinate stable states. Similarly, if an aggregate in nature is subjected to a heat source either within or outside the aggregate itself, the temperature might rise to such a point that the state of the ingredients changes with the consequence that the character of the aggregate is destroyed. But these possibilities are beside the point, for the machine model supposes parts put together that do not enter into either chemical or nuclear reactions or undergo changes of state. The position which holds that every entity in the universe is either an elementary particle or an arrangement of particles, implicitly--if not explicitly--maintains that interactions of the sort described do not occur. Both the stated position and the machine model require such a state of affairs.

One might be inclined to think that machines do show new behavioral capacities or properties because they can begin to operate once they are assembled. Machines do things that were not done before. Clocks keep time, automobiles travel down the street, electric drills bore holes, etc. But assembling a machine or applying it to some object is no more responsible for bringing about a new kind of property or operational capacity than any ordinary union of an agent or active power with its object. If the sun's rays are prevented from striking a block of ice by an insulating shield, removing the shield does not produce a new capacity for acting, it merely allows the agent to affect an object. The same is true when one puts a kettle on the stove; the agent is put in contact with an object it can heat, thereby bringing about its effect, but the putting of the kettle on the stove does not cause a new property or active capacity.

We may now summarize the points we have been making in the following way. A machine is an aggregate constituted principally by an external order that does not result in the modification of physical properties or bring about new behavioral abilities in its parts. Instead a machine is a medium which allows a natural agency to act on a passive recipient whose character is determined by the properties already present in it. Such motion or modification (electrification, a limited rise in temperature, etc.) is the only "new property" the machine has, except its human utility. Hence, if a natural stuff is an ordered aggregate, what we have just said will be true of it. On the other hand, if the set of properties belonging to the stuffs of the thing or its parts is changed other than through a change of state, then some sort of interaction over and beyond an external ordering has occurred; and such an entity is not an aggregate.

C. Elementary particles and atoms

We indicated above that atoms, like compounds, cannot be adequately described as aggregates of particles. Although atoms are described in terms of the numbers of protons, neutrons, and electrons that are required to make them, we cannot assume from this description that they are aggregates, that they are without interactions among the particles, for on that assumption we cannot explain the properties they have which the protons, neutrons, and electrons lack. But the case for atoms having properties their parts do not have is made thoroughly and in detail by Enrico Cantore, and we shall leave the presentation of this issue to him.[1]

D. Essentials of the argument recapitulated

Cast in a Figure II-EAE syllogism our argument is the following:

Major: No aggregate acquires new physical properties;
Minor: Every compound acquires new physical properties;
Conclusion: No compound is an aggregate.

The reader can see that the minor and major premisses have been discussed in this and the preceding chapter.

We also need a disjunctive argument that goes as follows:

Every stuff is either an aggregate or a substance;
Compounds are not aggregates;
Therefore compounds are substances.

Notes to Chapter 10

[1]See his *Atomic Order* (Cambridge, Massachusetts: The MIT Press, 1969). This, I think, is a fine book.

CHAPTER 11

PROPERTIES AND STRUCTURE

A. A difficulty

As we saw earlier, some philosophers have objected to substance on the grounds that it would have to be a bare particular devoid of any character of its own, functioning only as a carrier for the properties inhering in it. So although we have argued that a compound cannot be an aggregate, someone might object that we have not yet shown *different* substances to be involved in chemical changes. We must face the contention that although the set of properties of the compound is different from that of the elements, the substrata themselves are not different. And if that is true, then how can characterless particulars be distinguished according to kinds? How can one characterless substance be different from another characterless substance? In short, the objection contends that although different sets of properties appear and disappear in a chemical reaction, the substances themselves do not; for no distinction in kinds of substance is possible.

To reply to the objection we must first note that under the same conditions the set of properties which defines an element or a compound is constant; that is, under the same conditions we find the complete set appearing in many samples. We do not find samples in which one or two properties are replaced by others. This constancy tells us that the properties are in some way connected-- necessarily connected, we may say. But if different sets of

properties each reside in a featureless substratum, then how do we
account for the constant sets of properties? What is the nature of
the connection among the properties?

If we reflect, we can see that the possibilities for explaining the
connections are only two: (1) either properties are linked through
their substratum-substance, or (2) they are linked directly to one
another; there is no third alternative. If properties are linked
through the substratum-substance, then they must be rooted in it,
which means that, in addition to existing in the substance, they
have a causal origin within it. In this case no difficulties occur in
explaining them as a constant set. Since every property is
ultimately rooted in--not just sitting on--and caused by the
substance, the necessary concomitance is at once accounted for and
allows us to see why chemists spontaneously consider elements and
their compounds to be different substances. Furthermore, if
properties have causal roots within substances, then it follows that
substances are intrinsically knowable and are not bare particulars.
They have a knowability in themselves which is got at *through* the
properties but which is not identical to the knowability of the
properties. Stating the point another way, we may say that
properties make themselves known to us, and in addition they
throw light on something other than themselves, namely, the
interior of the substance. Just as an acceleration shows itself to us
and also tells us something about an extrinsic force, so, too,
properties tell us a little about the interior of the substance. To be
sure, beyond inferring that the properties have roots in the
substance and therefore the substance has a knowable "within," we
can say little. And if the natures of the properties are imperfectly
grasped, the natures of the roots are too. Nonetheless this state of
affairs does mean that different sets of properties imply genuinely
different substances as their substrata, no matter how imperfectly
the substrata might be known.

Nor does it matter whether the properties are ordered. That is,
if one property is rooted in another and that other is rooted in still
another and the last is rooted directly in the substance, then all the
properties are ultimately rooted in the substance, and the "within"
of the substance gives rise to them all. Now, however, let us turn
to the second possibility, which implies that the properties could
"sit" on the substance but not be rooted in it.

We must note at once that this amounts to saying that all
properties inhere contingently in substance; it amounts to holding

that the substance is indifferent to whether the properties are found in it or not, much as *sitting* is a property that can come and go in men, and as the shape of Hercules can come and go in clay. Yet if the properties of stuffs are always found together in sets, where is the connection among them? How are they connected?

If first we assume that one property is necessarily connected to another because one resides in and is rooted in the other property as a subject, we would have no reason whatever to deny that a property could be rooted in a substance. On the other hand, if properties are connected to one another without being grounded in the substance, then how is the connection effected?

If one property does not directly reside in another, then the two must be joined by a third reality, which would have to be either a property or a substance. If the properties were linked by a substance (but not as a subject), their union would be mechanical, a strange state of affairs indeed! And if they were linked by a property, the link would have to be through one property being a mechanical link to another (being a subject is excluded), and that would be stranger yet! The only other possibility is a necessary connection that would have to come from one property being an agent cause of another, which is not a plausible option either. Agents and movers involve either separate entities or separate parts. The properties in question are, however, always united and not related either as things or parts. It seems, then, that properties cannot be directly connected to one another without involving a substratum.

Furthermore, if a set of properties were directly linked, then chemical reactions would be a coming to be of properties that did not involve a substratum, which seems to suggest that the properties would come into existence out of nothing. But if properties are rooted in substance, then their coming to be is not out of nothing. Moreover, a change of substance is explicable. When the action of one substance directly modifies a property or properties of another, then given the necessary connections among properties that come from their necessary connections within the substance, it follows that changing the property entails changing the roots and hence the interior of the substance. Because the roots of properties are connected within a substance, changing the root of one property changes them all and thereby the entire "within" of the substance.

And so we must hold that properties depend upon roots in their subject for their existence; that is where we must look for the ground of their constant association with one another. Stated another way, we are forced to admit that a constant set of properties which inheres in a substance also stems from it, which is to say that the subject is not only passively related to the properties but actively as well; it is active not in the sense that the substance is an agent that acts to produce the property, but in the sense that the substance has *an actual root* of the property within it. The determinate existence and character of a property can depend upon only a determinate interior of the substance, not on an interior that is featureless or bare. From this we may conclude that substances are many in kind, for different sets of properties imply different sets of roots and so different interiors. Now, however, it is time to consider the priority of one property over others.

B. The structure among particles as a primary property

When we spoke of artefactual entities, especially machines, we argued that the artefactual structure is itself an extrinsically imposed (and so contingent) property that *presupposes* the natural physical properties of the materials ordered or arranged by it. An artefactual structure, because it is an extrinsically imposed order, does not and cannot endow materials with new physical properties. Yet when we listen to physicists and chemists, we hear them say that structure--what geologists call the "internal structure," not "external" form or shape--is the source of a stuff's other properties, which makes it appear that the position we have defended is not sound. It would seem that some structures do bring about new physical properties in stuffs. Furthermore, if such a structure is a source of properties, then a single molecule or atom would not have the properties of the whole. As a start, then, let us see what the current theory has to say about structure in the particles of substances and its role as a foundation for other properties.

The September 1967 issue of *Scientific American* was devoted to materials, and when the editors published that issue separately as a book, they wrote an introduction in which they said the following:

To make materials, atoms join together in the solid state. The great diversity of materials reflects essentially the fact that atoms come in different sizes and form bonds of greater or lesser strength and directionality with one another. Depending on their relative sizes and the nature of the bonds that engage them, atoms assemble in more or less tight, stable and regular structures. The atomic architecture of these structures determines the gross properties of each kind of material.[1]

Materials are made of atoms that join together to form solids. The great diversity of properties that characterize materials results, the editors tell us, from the atoms that bond together in more or less tight, stable, and regular structures, which determine the gross properties of each kind of material. An article by A.H. Cottrell in the same book, called "The Nature of Metals," is a bit more specific, spelling out a little more the relation between the structure and the other properties:

Metals are opaque, lustrous and comparatively heavy. They are strong, but they can be rolled or hammered into shape and can be alloyed and welded. They are good conductors of heat and electricity. All of these properties of metals flow from the metallic bond. The basis of the bond is that in a metal each atom is closely surrounded by many similar atoms, each with only a few electrons in its outer electron shell. In this situation the electron clouds overlap and loosely held outer electrons are so completely shared as to be no longer associated with individual atoms. Leaving the metal atoms in place as ions, they form an electron gas, a pervasive glue that moves freely among the atoms and bonds them together....

The metallic bond is nonspecific, which explains why different metals can be alloyed or joined one to another. It is also nondirectional, pulling equally hard in all directions. It therefore binds the metal atoms tightly so that their cores (nuclei and inner-shell electrons) fit closely among one another. The close packing favored by the metallic bond is best realized in certain regular crystalline structures. These structures, although resistant to tension, offer less resistance to shearing forces, and thus they explain the ductility of metals. They are by defini-tion dense, and thus they explain the comparative heaviness of metals. The mechanical properties of metals, then, derive from their crystalline structure, which is favored by the free-electron metallic bond.

Not only do we hear that structures account for properties, we are also told specifically which properties they explain. What, then, are we to say about such a structure?

As a start, let us consider the division of substances into parts. If we divide a macroscopic sample of a compound or element, for a time the parts have the properties of the whole sample; and clearly if we take the parts collectively, we then have some sort of aggregate, or so it would seem. We must, however, stop at molecules in dividing a compound and at atoms in dividing an element, since further divisions result in the substance ceasing to exist. It gets broken down into other stuffs--elements in the case of a compound, sub-atomic particles in the case of an atom--that are more elementary. In short, the molecules of a compound or the atoms of an element are *posterior* to the compound or to the element *insofar as they come to exist separately as minimum parts by division of the substance.* Atoms and molecules are indeed known that way--as resulting from a division of the whole--and so they are defined in relation to the whole. Nonetheless, there are other parts that are *prior* to the whole, parts upon which the nature of the whole depends; and *insofar as substances are made from prior constituents*--elements in the case of compounds, elementary particles in the case of atoms--*that have properties distinct from those of the whole that comes to be*, substances *cannot* be conceived as aggregates. That was the burden of our argument in an earlier chapter. Thus, to repeat the point we have been making, the physical properties of solids, liquids, and gases depend upon the bonding and the order among the particles of *the stuff that has come to be*, that is, the particles of the stuff that has the nature of the new substance. As chemists say, one atom (or molecule) is not a gas nor a liquid or solid. Stated another way, we may say that to be complete in species, a substance requires a plurality of particles. More importantly, however, the natural structure that orders atomic or molecular parts of a substance *springs from within the atoms or molecules themselves and depends on their kind.* So because the structure originates internally, we see why it can in a derivative way be a source of properties.   The point bears emphasis.

As we have said, a natural structure, unlike one that is artefactual, is rooted in the atoms or the molecules themselves. On that account, natural structures are *virtually*, if not actually, *in the molecules or atoms prior to their coming together in aggregation.* By no means can the ordered particles be likened to the parts of machines, which are passive recipients of an arrangement that is not rooted in the parts; hence the word "structure" is equivocal as it is applied to a structure of atoms on the one hand and an arrangement of a machine or any other aggregate of a similar type on the other.   We may say, then, that the natural atomic or molecular structure of a substance is its *first property*; it is a sort of medium for other properties that are rooted in the substance through it and is a kind of cause of them. That explains our being able to answer *why* a substance is ductile, etc., by describing its atomic or molecular structure.   In contrast, the structure of an artefact presupposes such natural structures in its materials together with the other accompanying properties. And so because an arrangement of atoms or molecules is the first property of a substance, we shall call the structure of atoms or molecules the "primary natural structure."

C. Secondary natural structures

Although we are repeating some things we said earlier, we must note that in addition to the structure which orders the atoms or molecules of a single substance, there is another that is different.   Consider, for instance, the structure of the earth. Geologists tell us that the earth's major parts are its core, mantle, and crust; and they also point out that these parts differ from one another by their density. At one time the earth was molten, and its liquid state allowed the substances of the mixture to settle according to their relative densities. In that way they acquired an order that was in part the effect of the liquid state and in part the effect of gravity. This sort of order can be said to be a secondary kind of natural structure, since it presupposes the different substances of the mixture and their relations to one another. And because the order is an arrangement of the heterogeneous parts, this secondary natural structure bears a resemblance to the structure of artefacts.

Speaking generally, heterogeneous mixtures are capable of assuming an order according to the forces that affect them; but if there is to be an enduring order imposed on a mixture, by whatever agency, the parts of the mixture must retain their nature and heterogeneity, that is, not undergo chemical reactions, including the ionization that occurs in many solutions. (Obviously if chemical reactions do occur, there may no longer be a heterogeneous mixture of any sort; or at least the mixture will be different.) So as we have indicated, we shall call such an order a "secondary natural structure." Finally, the geologists' use of "structure" to mean "crystalline form" (shape) is still another meaning, and the context shows when that sense is required. It ought not to be confused with the meanings given above.

D. The whole and its parts

The discussion we have just finished was undertaken in part for epistemological reasons that go beyond the ontological aim of describing the structure among atoms and molecules as a first property which is a causal medium between other properties and substance. The epistemological issue has to do with a division between the world of ordinary experience and that of science, a division that finds a home in many heads. It appears in a well known passage from Sir Arthur Eddington:

> As a conscious being I am involved in a story. The perceiving part of my mind tells me a story of a world around me. The story tells of familiar objects. It tells of colours, sounds, scents belonging to these objects; of boundless space in which they have their

existence, and of an ever-rolling stream of time bringing change and incident. It tells of other life than mine busy about its own purposes.

As a scientist, I have become mistrustful of this story. In many instances it has become clear that things are not what they seem to be. According to the story teller I have now in front of me a substantial desk; but I have learned from physics that the desk is not at all the continuous substance that it is supposed to be in the story. It is a host of tiny electric charges darting hither and thither with inconceivable velocity. Instead of being solid substance my desk is more like a swarm of gnats.

So I have come to realise that I must not put overmuch confidence in the story teller who lives in my mind. On the other hand, it would not do to ignore him altogether, since his story generally has some foundation of truth. . . .

Physical science deliberately aims at presenting a new version of the story of our experience from the very beginning, rejecting the familiar story as too erratic a foundation.

But although we try to make a clean start, rejecting instinctive or traditional interpretations of experience and accepting only the kind of knowledge which can be inferred by strictly scientific methods, we cannot cut ourselves loose altogether from the familiar story teller. We lay down the principle that he is always to be mistrusted; but we cannot do without him in science. What I mean is this: we rig up some delicate physical experiment with galvanometers, micrometers, etc., specially designed to eliminate the fallibility of human perceptions; but in the end we must trust to our perceptions to tell us the result of the experiment. Even if the apparatus is self-recording we employ our senses to read the records. So, having set the experiment going, we turn to the familiar story teller and say "Now put that into your story." He has perhaps just been telling us that the moon is about the size of a dinner plate, or something equally crude and unscientific;

but at our interruption he breaks off to inform us that
there is a spot of light coinciding with division No. 53
on the scale of our galvanometer. And this time we
believe him--more or less. At any rate we use this
information as the basis of our scientific conclusions.
If we are to begin actually at the beginning we must
inquire why we trust the story teller's information
about galvanometers in spite of his general
untrustworthiness. For presumably his fertile
invention is quite capable of "embroidering" even a
galvanometer.[2]

All of us are to some extent in the quandary that Eddington
describes. We confront the world in two ways, first on the basis of
ordinary experience, secondly on the theoretical grounds proposed
by modern science. And like Eddington, we might well wonder
about the connection between the two ways, perhaps, also like him,
mistrusting the evidence of ordinary experience.

But we are misled if we think the two are altogether disparate.
We are not obliged to choose one or the other; rather, we need to
understand that the scientific realm of theory is an attempt to
account for the realities we first come to know in our ordinary way.
Moreover, when we remember that properties are causally rooted
in substances, we see that the division of substances into particle-
parts determines how we account for the properties that belong to
the whole as such. In other words, we account for physical qualities
and other properties insofar as the substance has a multitude of
parts; for in the case of inanimate substances, the whole is the
quantity of the stuff. If we are given a certain order and bond-
strength between atomic or molecular parts which make the parts
relatively immobile with respect to each other, then we can account
for the solid state of the whole. On the other hand, if the parts are
only very loosely bonded, if the electrostatic forces among the
particles are weak, then we might expect the substance to be a gas.
In short, the scientific story tells us about the parts of substances
and how they are disposed in relation to the whole, a particular
disposition of the parts being required for certain other specific
properties to be present. So once again, the story told by science
informs us about sub-microscopic parts of the macroscopic wholes

they cause and which we first confront in ordinary life. On that account, Eddington's two stories are not incompatible.

E. Essentials of the arguments recapitulated

I. Properties are rooted in substance.

A. Disjunctive argument

1. The constancy of a set of properties results either from the properties being rooted in a substance or from the direct union of properties with one another (the disjunction is strict, it is not an alternative proposition);

2. The constancy does not result from the direct union of one property with another;

3. Therefore the constancy of a set of properties results from the properties being rooted in substance.

B. Disjunctive argument to establish (2) above

If (2) is not true:

Properties would be united either by one inhering in another as in a subject or by a third reality joining them.

If properties are united by one residing in another as in a subject, then they can reside in substance;

By assumption the consequent is denied.

If the properties are united directly (not through substance), then a third reality is required.

The consequent leads us back to the original problem and is no solution and so is denied.

Substance cannot be a mechanical (non-subject) link between properties:

Therefore (2) above is true, and (3) above is true.

II.   Knowability of substance

Substances contain causal roots of properties;
Therefore substances are intrinsically knowable.

III. **The natural structure is a primary property that is a medium through which other properties reside in substance**

Notes to Chapter 11

1Materials (San Francisco: W.H. Freeman and Company, 1967).

2New Pathways in Science (Cambridge: At the University Press, 1947), p. 2.

CHAPTER 12

PRIMARY NATURAL STRUCTURE
AND QUANTITY

A. Extension

Addressing structure in a more explicitly philosophical way, we wish to note that magnitude or extension (we use the words as synonyms) is a property of a thing or stuff. Extension itself is not, as some might have it, a substance; rather, extension tells us how much there is of the stuff, whether more or less, and it is in the category called "quantity." As we said earlier, "quantity" must not be confused with the current use of "quantitative" as describing any measurement of more or less.[1] But we need to consider the issue further.

When we consider magnitude, we understand that insofar as a body is extended it is potentially divisible into parts that are (spatially) exterior to one another; and bodies are divisible in three dimensions. These potential divisions make plain that within the whole we can "locate" parts both with respect to each other and with respect to the whole. Stated another way, the parts have "position" within the whole, which means that insofar as a body is extended, its physical parts have an order. If however, the precise relation of one part to another were to be specified, its "position" or "location" would have to be determined by reference to more or less precisely established coordinates associated with some part taken as a reference. So starting from what ordinary observation reveals, we may rightly describe extension as the order among the parts of a stuff or substance that are exterior to one another (they occupy a different space) and are united so as to form on the macroscopic level what we call a "continuum."

We must be careful not to mix up macroscopic realities with the theoretical models of atoms and molecules as particles with lots of space between them. Atoms and molecules are posulated to account for ordinary experience, and when we consider a body from the point of view of its being composed of atoms or molecules, we postulate bonds that unite the particles, introducing thereby an order among them which accounts for the macroscopic extension of the whole. And as we know, such an order is called an atomic or molecular "structure." But we can also see that the latter is equivalent to the extension, for both are the order of parts that are exterior to one another.

Of course not all stuffs are the same, for fluid bodies are characterized by the relative mobility of their parts within the whole, so the structure is not determinate in the way it is in solids. Yet atoms and molecules do give rise to an extended stuff when they are bonded together, different kinds of atoms or molecules giving rise to different sets of physical qualities accompanying the magnitude. The point needs elaboration.

B. Extension and other properties

When we reflect we see that, without extension, other properties cannot exist in a substance. For instance, liquid flow and gaseous diffusion, *which involve the relative movements of parts with respect to each other*, would be impossible, as would properties such as viscosity, ductility, breakableness, conductivity, etc., all of which also involve the reference of one part to another. Thus, real substances require a number of particles--in principle at least more than one--*to exist as something complete in species*; that is, *to exist as something that has all the properties which characterize and define the stuff.* In contrast, a single particle--an atom or molecule--seems to be somewhat like a bodily organ taken by itself, which, although it is a part of an animal, is incomplete insofar as the whole nature of the animal does not show itself in the part. Analogously but not identically, a solitary atom does not actually have all the properties of the substance, though it does have them virtually insofar as through aggregation of the atoms the properties can exist in the substance. Only by reason of this virtual possession can an atom or molecule be said to be the smallest part of the substance "that retains the properties of the whole." (In perhaps a more fundamental way, elementary particles would seem to be incomplete in species. Just as an arm is not a man, so an electron, proton, etc., would seem not to be a complete substance; they seem to be by nature parts, just as an arm is a part. But these are theoretical entities, and one can only conjecture.)

Metaphorically we might say that natural substances are "social" by nature insofar as they require multitudes of particles for the properties of the substance to exist. Atoms and molecules do lose their identity in the whole, their latent individuality appearing only when a substance becomes active with respect to another or when the substance is affected by another, the most obvious instance being chemical activity. So once again, because all other properties presuppose extension, atomic or molecular structure is the primary property of the substance, one through which other properties are enabled to exist in the substance.

Of course even when atoms and molecules exist by themselves they do have properties, and nothing we have said is intended to suggest they do not. Physicists do speak of some atoms and molecules as larger and others as smaller, and they also talk about atomic diameters. Atoms and molecules have mass, a total charge, movements, etc.; so when we say that extension is necessary for the physical properties of the whole stuff, we do not intend to say that isolated atoms and molecules are unextended. Plainly they are not; but unless there is more than one atom or molecule, unless the substance has a minimum magnitude, the physical properties cannot exist; that is our point.

C. A summary and overview

Natural substances that are complete in species have all the properties which define the most obviously characteristic samples; and because the physical properties (as well as others) presuppose extension or quantity, a substance that is complete in species is extended, which means that it must contain more than one particle. An analogous state of affairs obtains with respect to the atom itself and the particles of which it is composed. Thus we may say that in an extended sense of the term material particles are social by nature. But having considered (along with the several senses of "structure") the order among atoms or molecules that constitutes the extension or quantity of a stuff together with what follows from the structure, we shall make a few other summary remarks for the sake of providing an overview of aggregates before we undertake the issue to be discussed in the next chapter.

First let us recall that chemical reactions produce a new substance, not an aggregate. The substance produced has a set of properties that differs from the set found in any of the reactants, yet the compound is *generically* the same kind of substance as its composing elements; that is, the compound is a homogeneous stuff, either solid or fluid, ductile, viscous conductive, etc.,and it can undergo both physical and chemical changes. In other words, the behavior as well as the properties of a compound are of *the same kinds* as those of the elements composing it.

Another important point about inanimate stuffs is that a whole sample of an element or compound which is active (for example, it may heat or radiate) does not act on itself but on another sample that is extrinsic to it, just as a single molecule or atom does not act on itself but on another atom or molecule. In short, activity and passivity are spatially divided in things that are inanimate precisely because the molecular or atomic parts are all the same. So just as one molecule or atom cannot affect itself, so neither can an accumulation of them.

Yet another point needs to be repeated here: the arrangement or structure that would constitute an aggregate that is a property-thing is distinct in kind from the structure stemming from atoms and molecules and which is the first property of a substance, namely, quantity. The order of parts of a true aggregate does not allow chemical interaction, otherwise new compounds would be formed and the aggregate would lose its character. The order of an aggregate will allow bonding of distinct kinds of particles (through Van der Waals forces, for example), and a physical activity of one part on another; but that is all. In short, the very notion of natural aggregate precludes interactions other than those of a physical, non-chemical or non-nuclear sort. Only under such conditions can a natural aggregate resemble a machine and be an arrangement in the mechanistic sense.

Notes to Chapter 12

[1]*Quantity* is a universal genus or category containing two immediate subdivisions: *magnitude* or extension, which we are now discussing, and *homogeneous multitude*, such as 10 apples, 12 horses, etc.

CHAPTER 13

WHETHER ORGANISMS ARE AGGREGATES

A. Introduction

Although we have argued that chemical compounds are not aggregates, other questions remain. Ludwig Von Bertalanffy, speaking for himself as well as others, claims that substances are homogeneous. So because organisms are heterogeneous, organized system, they do not appear to be substances. And though Von Bertalanffy has attacked the contention that organisms can be likened to machines, even he appears to regard them as aggregates of compounds. Of course a natural aggregate is not the product of human manufacture, yet it is constituted solely by an ordering of materials, which means we must ask whether the distinguishing characteristics of living things can be accounted for by an ordering of parts to make a property-whole. In other words, there are many who implicitly if not explicitly admit compounds to be substances but deny that organisms are. Hence we must consider as a separate question, whether organisms are only highly organized systems of compounds whose properties can without addition be explained by physics and chemistry.

George Gaylord Simpson makes some remarks that highlight the issue rather well:

Living things are certainly different from the
nonliving in requiring these special modes of
explanation--functional and evolutionary. ...

What, then, is the difference between matter,
living and nonliving? It is the way the matter is
organized or put together. The elements of matter
that make up rocks, soil, air, and water are nitrogen,
oxygen, hydrogen, carbon, potassium, sodium, and
many others. These same elements are what we find
when we analyze the living organism. Here,
however, they are complexly combined and arranged
in a fashion never encountered in the nonliving
world. Put together in just the right way, these
elements form a system--*an organism*--that possesses
new capacities: growth and reproduction. The
organism *grows* by feeding on nonliving materials
and incorporating them into its characteristic
organization. Complex and fragile, the individual
organism always dies, but before it does, it
reproduces; it leaves a copy of itself.[1]

According to Simpson, organisms are "complexly combined and
arranged" elements found in rocks, soil, air, etc., and at the same
time they "possess new capacities." The question, then, is: are
these two claims compatible?

B. Organisms and structure

It is plain that organisms have distinct parts with distinct
functions and that the parts are spatially separated and spatially
related by a structure which allows the functions to be coordinated.
The text that follows describes organisms well from the point of
view of this coordination:

As everyone knows, order is the fixed arrangement
present in the existing constitution of things. Order
may also be considered as a sequence or succession in

space or time. Biological order is all that, and it is
especially a sequence in space *and* time. Biological
order is dual, structural and functional, static and
dynamic. Structural and functional orders are the
complementary aspects of living beings. A living
being is a dual system of order.[2]

Without being anatomists we know that on the macroscopic level
the skeletal system is distinct from the muscular system, the
circulatory system is distinct from both, the digestive system in its
turn is distinct from the others, etc. Furthermore, each system is
divided into its own spatially separated parts, as for example, the
esophagus, the stomach, the small and large intestine. So because
organisms do have an external structure they resemble machines
in a very important way and appear to be ordered aggregates.
André Lwoff gives us the following description:

The simplest organism is . . . a relatively complex
machine. All known complex systems which contain
macromolecules and are able to reproduce their kind
belong to the living systems. Reproduction of a
complex system containing macromolecules is
therefore characteristic of life. And such a complex,
independent unit of integrated structures and
functions that reproduces true to type can only be an
organism, a living organism.[3]

Let us observe at once that the structures of organs are accounted
for by their functions; "form follows function" says the biologist.
But if the mechanists are right, an organism can have no function
that would require more than an ordering of chemical compounds;
it could have no function that involved more than an application of
chemical reactions and physical changes. The center of focus, then,
has to be the character of biological activities.

C. The activities of organisms

Speaking of living things, Lwoff tells us how their activities differ from those of non-living things:

> A molecule is the smallest unit quantity of matter which can exist by itself and retain all the properties of the original substance. A molecule can be split into fragments, but each fragment is necessarily different from the original structure. Molecules might aggregate, but a molecule cannot divide. Neither can a molecule grow. Thus the growth and division of a bacterium is not the growth and division of its molecules.[4]

For his comparison of the living to the non-living he chooses the unicellular organism in the category of the living and the molecule in the category of the non-living. Cells divide to produce two *like* units, whereas if molecules divide, they produce *unlike* constituents. More generally, a cell can reproduce, grow, and maintain itself by assimilating nutrients, none of which can be done by a molecule. So it follows, says Lwoff, that "the growth and division of a bacterium [a unicellular organism] is *not* the growth and division of its molecules." In short, the properly biological operations belong to the cell as a whole insofar as it is a distinct unit, a point upon which Von Bertalanffy insisted. But the operations must be examined more closely.

To begin let us note that the three biological activities necessarily occur together. If an entity reproduces by a process of division, then it *must* also be able to grow, which gives us two activities. A consideration of the alternative makes the point plain; for if we suppose that mitosis could occur without growth, then after a limited number of divisions the dividing cells would contain too little material for further divisions. Hence in order that an organism maintain an adequate size, it must grow after it has divided. Even in large, multicellular animals and plants, there is a size (within variable limits) that is commensurate with mature operation.

But organisms must also have a third, nutritive activity to convert and assimilate food materials and assimilate them into the stuffs out of which their parts are maintained and made. Growth is an increase in the magnitude and the mass of the unit (we can ignore other aspects of an organism's growth here). And although the increase cannot occur without assimilating materials from outside, assimilation is not merely an accretion, such as that which occurs when a crystal "grows." Consequently the ability to reproduce entails both the ability to grow and the ability to assimilate. And because reproduction is the goal of the other two activities, it is very appropriately the operation through which *organism* is defined. With these points now in mind, can we say that reproduction is no more than an ordered series of physical and chemical activities?

D. Cell parts and cell division

A single cell that is an entity by itself and not a part of a larger whole is called a "unicellular organism," and looking at reproduction as it is found in it will make our task uncomplicated yet adequate for the matters at issue. For the sake of the readers who might be unfamiliar with mitosis, let us begin with a short description.[5]

The principal parts of a typical cell are (1) the nucleus, and (2) the cytoplasm, which surrounds the nucleus. These two major parts are contained by a membrane. Within the cytoplasm there are a number of compartments, as one source has it, called "organelles," that are the functioning parts of the cytoplasm. Some of the organelles are fixed in place (because they are formed from the outer membrane), while others are suspended in the fluid medium of the cytoplasm and can move around in it. Some principal organelles are (1) the endoplasmic reticulum, (2) mitochondria, (3) ribosomes, (4) Golgi apparatus, (5) lysosomes, and (6) centrioles. (Chloroplasts are important organelles found in plants.)

The endoplasmic reticulum consists of interconnected, folded sheets, formed from the cell membrane, that are sites of protein molecule synthesis. Mitochondria are threadlike, cylindrical bodies in which certain chemical reactions important for providing energy occur. Ribosomes are particles scattered around the

cytoplasm, some of which are free and some of which are attached
to the endoplasmic reticulum; they are sites of protein assembly.
The Golgi apparatus is an organelle formed from the cell
membrane, and it secretes proteins. Lysosomes are vesicular
bodies that contain powerful digestive enzymes. Centrioles are
bodies from which spindle fibers extend during mitosis. Now this
list is not complete, and the functions of the organelles are
minimally described, but we need not be more detailed or more
technical for the issue at hand. Let us consider, then, reproduction
as an activity.

Cell division is an activity originating within the cell--cells are
not divided by outside agencies--that produces two daughter cells of
the same type. The division of the cell as a whole requires the
division of its major parts, the nucleus and the cytoplasm. (The
division of the nucleus is properly called "mitosis," whereas the
division of the cytoplasm is called "cytokinesis," but we shall follow
a common practice and use "mitosis" to refer to the entire division.)
Before the nucleus divides, the chromosomes, which are the
principal parts of the nucleus, duplicate to form two complete sets.
The sets then separate from each other and become two nuclei,
following which the cytoplasm also divides to give two complete
cells. Separation of the chromosomes is brought about by spindle
fibers that extend out from the centrioles, attaching to the
chromosomes and pulling them in opposite directions so that two
distinct nuclei can be produced. The fibers are constructed for their
purpose at the appropriate time, and disintegrate when their task
is finished.

When the cytoplasm divides, the mitochondria divide too, so
that each cell has its share of them. Other organelles, such as
ribosomes, disintegrate during cytokinesis and are reformed once
cell division has been completed. Thus, we see in a general way
that cell division involves duplicating some parts and "parcelling
out (by disintegration and reconstruction)" others. Furthermore,
this reproductive activity belongs to the whole insofar as the
activity is initiated from within the whole and insofar as the whole
is separated into two distinct but like unit entities.

Let us now consider, by comparing the functions of the two,
whether a cell can be an ordered aggregate in the likeness of a
machine. First let us make the obvious point that unicellular
reproduction is not a "tool-activity" useful for some human
operation or the operation of any other organism; that is not its

generically new property. Rather, unicellular reproduction is for the advantage of the *species* of the reproducing unit, while the subordinate functions of growth and self-maintenance are for the advantage of the cell itself, enabling it to reproduce. Machines, however, neither improve themselves nor perpetuate their "species." Furthermore, a machine dedicated to making replicas of itself would not do so by dividing itself, and it would be without point.

Second, the function for which a machine is made is realized in its "output part or parts," namely, in the part or parts which do not act on any other, as the driving wheels of an automobile, the hands of a clock, the screen of a television set. Moreover, the function of a machine results from a serial movement, from a causal chain; so if a unicellular organism were an ordered aggregate, its function would occur in the same way and be located in an "output part." More specifically, since unicellular reproduction is a *division*, if a cell were an aggregate, an active part would divide a passive part in imitation of the causality of machines. Again, an active part would divide a passive part in a kind of cleavage or cutting, the required passive quality being either breakableness or sectility. Furthermore, although one active part would divide another, there would not be two identical units. The point bears emphasis.

As we saw earlier, though physical properties are active or passive, no such active property brings about an effect *within that which has the property*. Neither the sun nor a flame heats itself but something else; a body with mass does not attract itself, nor does a charged body attract or repel itself. When we speak of the parts of a natural body affecting one another by heat conduction, electrical conduction, gravitational attraction, etc., the active part does not affect itself but another that is passive. We made this point earlier when we observed that activity in the inanimate realm requires a system of two entities, one of which acts on the other. But now back to cells.

Whatever we might say about mitosis, it is not the division of one part by another; it is not the result of the kind of system found in the realm of inanimate things; that is, one organelle does not act on another organelle to divide it. To be sure, there are ordered movements and reactions in a cell that are serial and can be described as a causal chain, a matter we shall take up explicitly in a later chapter. At the moment we need only note that the causal chain does not terminate in the division by one organelle of another as an "output part," which is what the ordered aggregate view requires. A cell contains a directive principle that in some fashion replicates itself by distributing its parts into two like wholes. Hence our main point: if we take the mechanistic position at face value, no cell can be an ordered aggregate. But the case can be further strengthened.

E. Classification

The changes that occur in elements and compounds are, as has been said, either physical or chemical; these are the admitted categories. Furthermore, this classification is both natural and exhaustive in the realm of inanimate entities because it is founded upon the real distinction between substance and property. Physical changes are modifications of properties, whereas chemical changes are modifications of substances, that is, they effect the coming to be and passing away of new *kinds* of substances, and so the two kinds of change are mutually exclusive. (Nuclear reactions are not chemical reactions, of course, but they produce the same kind of effect: different substances. Instead of bringing about different compounds, they bring about different chemical elements.) On the other hand, when we consider cell division we see that it cannot be classified either in the category of chemical change as bringing about a new kind of substance or in the category of physical change as producing only changes of qualities. A chemical reaction produces end products that differ from the reactants--different molecules or atoms--whereas mitosis produces individuals of the same *kind*. Neither is autocatalysis the same as mitosis, for in autocatalysis a second molecule comes about because a first molecule of the same kind catalyses outside itself a second molecule's production: autocatalysis is not the division of a molecule into two like molecules. And repeating another point, we cannot say that cell division is a physical change, except in an equivocal sense; for the whole amount of stuff of the cell is divided from within, not from without.

It is perhaps important to repeat that mitosis admittedly cannot occur without physical and chemical changes taking place. A complete description of mitosis would involve quite a list of such processes. But this is not the point at issue. A physical change terminates in the modification of a property or properties, whereas a chemical change terminates in a new compound with a new set of properties. Cell division, however, terminates at neither. The two daughter cells resulting from mitosis are qualitatively alike and individual members of the same species. The activity whereby this effect is brought about is what is at issue, and it is sui generis. There is nothing like it in the categories of physical change and chemical change.

And so we may conclude that reproduction (not to mention growth and self-maintenance) gives rise to *a distinct category of activity*. Reproduction is the coming to be of a new individual substance that is not different in kind from its progenitor. It therefore issues from a distinct *kind* of behavioral capacity that cannot be classified with any of the active or passive physical properties. Reproduction is a new kind of behavior, which biologists generally admit, that shows the existence of a different kind of capacity or potentiality or behavioral disposition, whichever term one prefers.

F. Operations and their roots in substance

When we discussed whether compounds are aggregates, we argued that a characteristic set of properties is rooted within the substance itself. The substance is not just a passive carrier of the properties, it is also the causal source from which the properties stem. But if properties are rooted in substance, then activities or operations are even more so and for the same reason: operations cannot be directly connected to other operations and properties apart from a substance. More determinately, an aggregate cannot give rise to a new kind of behavioral capacity precisely because the aggregate is constituted by an order imposed on existing materials, and the order cannot be the immediate source of a new operation. Thus if *an external structure cannot modify physical properties, it is even less able to bring about new operational capacities.* Once more: the order itself cannot be the subject of a new capacity because the order is no more than an external relation of one thing to another. Furthermore, since cell division implies the concomitant occurrence of two additional operations, all three have to be grounded in substance. If they were not, we would be faced with an alternative similar to the one we rejected in regard to properties, namely, necessary connections among operations that are transient properties, none of which would have a cause within a substance.

G. Essential arguments recapitulated

Our principal case has now been made, so by way of a summary let us note first that the argument for mechanism depends at bottom on an argument by analogy: just as the operations of machines are accounted for by an ordering of predetermined parts, so, too, the operations of organism are accounted for by an ordering or arrangement of organic compounds. We argued against the position (by destroying the similarity) in arguments that can be stated as follows:

Chapter 14:

No aggregate manifests a new kind of behavioral capacity;
Every organism manifests a new kind of behavioral capacity;
Therefore no organism is an aggregate.

This syllogism was preceded by one that is similar:

Chapter 10:

No aggregate manifests new physical properties;
Every compound manifests new physical properties;
Therefore no compound is an aggregate.

Earlier we made the point that things are of two kinds: property-things (aggregates are a subdivision) and substantial things; there is no third alternative. On those grounds we constructed the following disjunctive arguments:

Chapter 14:

Every thing is either a property-thing or a substantial thing;
Organisms are not property-things;
Therefore organisms are substantial things (substances).

Another disjunctive argument was given for compounds:

Chapter 10:

Every stuff is either an aggregate or a substance;
Compounds are not aggregates;
Therefore compounds are substances.

Notes to Chapter 13

[1]George Gaylord Simpson, Colin S. Pittendrigh, and Lewis A. Tiffany, *Life* (New York: Harcourt, Brace and Company), Inc., 1957.

[2]André Lwoff, *Biological Order* (Cambridge, Massachusetts: MIT Press, 1968), p. 9.

[3]Ibid., p. 4.

[4]Ibid., p. 7.

[5]The description that follows contains only the most common statements one might make about organelles, but what we say is representative. The reader can check any physiology or histology text, as well as others.

CHAPTER 14

SENSATION, MIND, AND BODY: THE PROBLEM

A. Introduction

The preceding chapter argued that organisms are substances on the grounds that reproduction is a kind of operation not found in non-living things. The chapters to come will argue that organisms which are able to sense constitute still another kind of material substance, and they will argue on similar grounds, namely, that sensation is an operation distinct from reproduction, growth, and self-maintenance. The general principle is: substances that exhibit distinct kinds of operations are distinct substances.

The operation upon which we shall primarily focus in this and the next chapter will be external sensation, which means that our consideration will exclude many mental phenomena. By so limiting ourselves and by using seeing and hearing as examples, we omit the internal awareness of the sensation itself, as well as imagining, remembering, believing, aching, hurting, and other affective states. We shall also omit the notion of intentionality, for the term has not been uniformly understood in the history of philosophy; nor is it required for what we shall do. There is no need to embrace all that "mental" and its synonyms have come to suggest in current philosophical discussions.

Nor will it be maintained here that because sensation is a distinct kind of operation it requires its own spiritual substance; we shall not maintain a dualist position. Even if we grant that thinking is a peculiarly human activity, we cannot argue to a Cartesian position; its *uniqueness* does not establish that thinking requires a separately existing spiritual substance attached to a body that is external. So to repeat: by showing that sensation is a distinct kind of operation we shall have established only that there exists yet another kind of material substance; some organisms are sentient and others are not.

But our argument will bring us up against the claims of contemporary materialists; for not only do they argue against dualism, they also say that sensation is essentially no more than a physico-chemical activity, and in so doing they make sentient organisms to be material aggregates. The materialist view (other than dialectical materialism) is not only anti-dualist, it is also mechanistic and implies that sentient entities are adequately characterized as arrangements of inanimate materials. So although the last chapter sufficed to show that no organism-- including those that are sentient--is an aggregate, it will still be useful to consider sensation separately in the general context of the mind-body problem for the sake of distinguishing yet another kind of substance.

B. The issue stated

Over the last twenty years or so, the mind-body problem has been treated in a number of well known essays, which, despite certain differences, maintain together that mental phenomena are identical with brain processes; and the position common to them has come to be called the "mind-brain identity theory." In describing it, C. V. Borst says in his introduction to a collection of essays:

> The view is, as the name suggests, that mental states are quite literally identical with brain states: any given mental state is roughly, a brain state, brain process or feature of a process in the central nervous system.[1]

As Borst puts it, the position is straightforward: mental state and brain state are the same reality. And if this were so, no operational distinction of substantial entities could be founded on sensation, since "mental" includes sensation under its signification and can be taken to be representative.

Michael Levin, another author of materialist convictions,[2] states the thesis at greater length, claiming that altogether there are three possible positions on the mind-body problem, the first of which is:

(1) There are both mental and physical entities.

Levin construes this to mean that there are both physical and non-physical substances as well as physical and non-physical properties, a position that is both a substance dualism and a property dualism:

> It would be absurd to adopt [the position above] without endowing non-physical substances with some non-physical properties.

Historically this has been known as Cartesian dualism. The second position Levin presents is:

(2) There are only physical entities but some physical entities have both physical and non-physical, psychological properties.

This is taken to be "substance monism" along with "property dualism," and we shall understand the latter term to mean that there are "more than one category of properties, some of which are non-physical." This position is also opposed by materialists. The third and last is:

(3) There are only physical entities, and all properties of physical entities are physical.

Levin regards this position as both "substance monism" and "property monism," and takes it to represent the materialist view. But though these various materialist theories are fundamentally the same, not all account for the mental in the same way; so our task now will be to describe some of them well enough to consider their salient features and the various points that have to be taken into account.

C. Identity theories

The holders of the several identity theories say that they are proposing hypotheses to account for a correlation between the use of the expressions "mental act" or "mental phenomenon" on the one hand and "brain process" on the other. The first (1) form of the theory we shall discuss takes its inspiration from Frege's well known views on sense and reference as illustrated by the names "morning star" and "evening star," both of which refer to the planet Venus. Although the names applied to the planet are different, their referent, the planet, is the same; and so although the names "mental phenomenon" and "brain process" are different, their referent, like Venus, is held to be the same.

A second form (2) of the theory is said to be reductionist; it holds, for example, that "heat" or "temperature" on the one hand and "molecular motion" on the other are identical in the sense that temperature is reduced to molecular motion.[3] The third form (3), also said to be reductionist, differs in its inspiration; and it is illustrated by three examples in which two expressions are used for one reality. "Water" and "H_2O" signify the same reality, as do "lightning" and "atmospheric electrical discharge." Seen in the light of these examples, "sensation" would correspond to "water" and "lightning," whereas "brain process" would correspond to "H_2O" and "atmospheric electrical discharge." So now having briefly indicated the basic forms of the identity theory, we must look at them more closely.

D. The first view: sense and reference

The first position (1) claims that "brain process" and "mental phenomenon" refer to the same reality in the way in which "morning star" and "evening star" refer to the planet Venus. To evaluate the claim let us first note that these two expressions name or signify the same planet from two different properties, namely, its relative position and appearance in the morning and its relative position and appearance in the evening. That which is named in each case is, however, the planet itself, *whereas that from which the names are taken are properties*. Furthermore, the properties are distinct not only from each other but also from the subject in which they are found. We could call Socrates "that grammarian" and "that carpenter" and have the same sort of "identification"; for the arts of carpentry and grammar which are found in Socrates are different from each other and from the Socrates they name. As the medieval Aristotelians said, the two properties are *identical in subject*, but they are *formally distinct*. In contrast, *medicine* and the *art of healing the sick* are formally identical; and that helps us to see that when a thing is named from two properties there is no formal identity, either between one property and the other or between the properties and their subject. So, if the identity theory is willing to settle for saying that mental act and brain process have an identical subject, it has not carried the day; for such an identity is implicitly conceded from the start by many who are not dualists but who hold that a mental act is not a brain process. An identity of subject is compatible with formally distinct properties, even properties that are categorically distinct. On that account the identity theory has to contend that *mental act* and *brain process* are formally identical. (Certainly the properties are not taken as formally identical with the subject.)

As is now plain, the morning star account would seem to identify two properties because they inhere in the same subject, an error that probably would not occur if the real distinction between property and substance were taken into account by those who propose this position. Moreover, if a proponent of the identity view were to deny that a mental act and a brain process are distinct properties, then he could not hold that "mental phenomenon" and "brain process" are like "morning star" and "evening star." Instead he must hold the realities named to be formally identical; he must hold that the two names signify the same reality, either because they are synonyms or because one expression is related to the other as a definition is related to that which it defines in the way that the *art of healing the sick* is related to *medicine*.

E. The second view (2): properties and particles that are parts of a subject

The use of statistical mechanics to account for heat phenomena is considered by many to be a paradigm case in which reduction has been successfully carried out:

> I shall assume that the reduction of temperature to mean kinetic energy is one of the most plausible examples of theoretical reduction.[4]

Reducing temperature to mean kinetic energy is taken to establish their identity, and that is the issue: whether temperature or heat is the motion of particles.

To begin, let us note that in ordinary life when we speak of temperature we speak of a quality we call "hot," and the word "temperature" signifies that quality insofar as it can be more or less intense and therefore subject to measurement. We take the quality to be a real property of things, so it is not a surprise to find another author saying about this type of reduction:

> [The layman] is assured by some authorities he now consults that the individual molecules of a gas cannot be said to possess a temperature, and that the meaning of the word is identical "by definition" with the meaning of 'the mean kinetic energy of molecules.' Confronted by such apparently conflicting ideas, he may therefore find a host of typically "philosophical" questions both relevant and inescapable.[5]

It seems that temperature has been "reduced" by definition to mean the molecular motion which accounts for it because the reality of the property has been denied; and so the ordinary man

> is confronted with a serious issue as to what is genuine "reality" and what is only appearance.[6]

He is led to say that his experience bears on an appearance and not on the real. That is the view of the late Sir Arthur Eddington who in some well known lines quoted earlier told us that we can choose between two desks:

> As a conscious being I am involved in a story. The perceiving part of my mind tells me a story of a world around me. The story tells of familiar objects. It tells of colours, sounds, scents belonging to objects; of boundless space in which they have their existence, and of an ever-rolling stream of time bringing change and incident. It tells of other life than mine busy about its own purposes.
>
> As a scientist I have become mistrustful of this story. In many instances it has become clear that things are not what they seem to be. According to the story teller I have not in front of me a substantial desk; but I have learned from physics that the desk is not all the continuous substance that it is supposed to be in the story. It is a host of tiny electric charges darting hither and thither with inconceivable velocity. Instead of being solid substance my desk is more like a swarm of gnats.[7]

Eddington thinks that the perceiving part of his mind presents him with an illusion because the "swarm of gnats" do not have the properties of the "substantial desk." One is appearance and the other reality.[8] And so if mental act and brain process on the one hand and temperature and molecular motion on the other are parallel to Eddington's two desks, then the materialist will construe a mental act to be at best an appearance of some sort, and brain process the reality. But this, we think, is not the right view of the matter.

In an earlier chapter we noted that the physical properties of an amount of stuff depend on the molecules or atoms that come together to form the whole. Because such properties presuppose extension they do not occur in individual molecules, hence we must distinguish the parts from the whole they compose. Even when a property attributed to the whole is the same in kind as the one attributed to its parts, the two properties are often different. Consider, for instance, a golf ball just driven from a tee. The flight of the ball describes a parabola that can be represented on a graph. But if we were to superimpose on that graph the paths of the individual molecules, we would expect to find that none of the graphs for the molecules corresponded exactly to the trajectory of the golf ball. And although someone might claim that the motion of the golf ball is the statistical average of the motion of its molecules, we may reply that this in effect concedes the point. The numbers representing the motion of the whole might represent a calculational average, but the motion itself is not an average. Every average is by definition a mathematical result which is not expected to correspond to any single entity, even though in some cases by accident it might. In short, molecules are parts of a whole and move within it but are not individually endowed with the precise motion that characterizes the whole.

We know that a whole is not the same as its parts, even though the whole depends on them. Furthermore, it is essential to remember that despite much of what has been said apropos of theoretical entities, they are indeed postulated *to account for what we observe*. Theoretical entities are put forward by the mind as a tentative and correctible explanation of that which experience makes known to us. Consequently, we can have both of Eddington's desks; we are not obliged to pick between them. The desk we know by ordinary experience is a macroscopic whole endowed with properties for which our theories propose a cause in the form of a "swarm of gnats." On that account, there can be no "reduction" of temperature to molecular motion, for that would mean that temperature *is* the molecular motion, not a quality of the whole *caused* by it. Moreover, when we felt something hot *we would feel moving particles*, if that were what the quality hot is; and that would be true whether we hold the quality *hot* to exist only in the sensory power or whether we hold it to exist in the thing. Strictly speaking, Rumford was not correct when he said, "Heat is motion." He should have said, "Heat is caused by the motion of the particles of a stuff," and that is probably what he meant. So we do not have a case of genuine identity, since the parts of the whole which explain a property or properties are not identical with the property or properties themselves. This point is explicitly conceded by Nagel, who, although he regards the example above as an instance of reduction, states:

> The essential point in this discussion is that in the reduction of thermodynamics to mechanics a postulate connecting temperature and mean kinetic energy of gas molecules must be introduced, and that this postulate cannot be warranted by simply explicating the meanings of the expressions contained in it.[9]

If reduction requires a postulate that cannot be justified by the meanings of the terms it contains, then what it connects must be distinct and not identical.

F. The third view (3): formal identity

The third position, the reader will recall, is illustrated by the examples "water"and "H_2O," as well as "lightning" and "atmospheric electrical discharge." Just as each of these pairs of terms signifies the same reality, so, it is said, do "mental act" and "brain process." The illustrations are genuine cases of formal identity, for "water" and "H_2O" signify the same reality, as do "lightning" and "atmospheric electrical discharge." Nonetheless the members of the pairs are not altogether the same, for "water" signifies the stuff obscurely, whereas "H_2O" signifies it more distinctly, since it is a definition given in terms of the stuff's constituents. If we ask "What is water?" we will get the reply, "A compound substance composed of two parts hydrogen and one part oxygen." "H_2O" is its shorthand expression and is especially suitable for chemical equations. A similar relation exists between "lightning" and "atmospheric electrical discharge," though in this case the definition is not complete enough for strict explanations. We may summarize our remarks by saying that in each case one expression is a definition and the other a name for the same reality. However, despite the formal identity on the part of that which is signified, the expressions themselves are not equivalent; for one signifies obscurely and the other more clearly. Without question we understand more through one than through the other.

From these considerations it now becomes plain that if "mental act" and "brain process" are formally identical in relation to what they signify, then *brain process* will have to function as the definition of *mental act*; and our task will have to be to determine whether that is so.

Notes to Chapter 14

[1]C. V. Borst, ed., *The Mind-Brain Identity* Theory (London: Macmillan and Co. Ltd., 1970).

[2]*Metaphysics and the Mind-Body Problem* (Oxford: Clarendon Press, 1979), p. 50.

[3]Our only interest in reduction here is in the cases before us which are presented as instances of identity that do away with the mental as a distinct kind of property.

[4]James W. Cornman, *Materialism and Sensations* (New Haven and London: Yale University Press, 1971), p. 63.

[5]Ernest Nagel, *The Structure of Science* (New York: Harcourt, Brace & World, Inc., 1961), p. 342.

[6]Ibid.

[7]*New Pathways in Science* (Cambridge: At the University Press, 1947), p. 1.

[8]"Appearance" is of course ambiguous. Sometimes it means "that which appears but is illusory"--the sense Eddington employs--and at other times it means "the observable properties (that are distinct from the stuff)."

[9]Op. cit., p. 357.

CHAPTER 15

SENSATION AS AN ACTIVITY: ITS CHARACTER

A. Guidelines for our considerations

Discussions of the mind-body problem often employ illustrations that are unusual or obscure rather than those that are regular or more evident; we are all familiar with the "orange after-image," which is a case in point. Moreover, those who identify the mental with brain processes do not describe the latter, even in its essentials. Our own presentation therefore will attempt to avoid both shortcomings; first, as we said in the previous chapter, by making external sensation our point of focus, and second, by describing in its essentials (not in all its details) the brain process with which sensation would be identified. Such an approach would appear both more empirical and more systematic. It also makes unnecessary an extensive recapitulation of current literature, which would be both impractical and out of place. In summary, then, the following will be done:

a. the mental will be represented by external sensation;
b. the physiological process involved in sensation will be described in its essentials;
c. our own critique will be made on the basis of the substance-property distinction that has already been established.

B. Sensations and impulses

If *brain process* is identical to sensation, then sensation is indeed a physiological process, and the electrical activities--the impulses--that occur in nerve cells *are* sensations. This is the first proposition we must examine.[1]

Brain processes are essentially the same as the processes that occur elsewhere in neural tissue. All neural tissue contains nerve cells or neurons, which carry impulses that pass to other neurons through connections called "synapses." Because the impulse depends upon moving charges, to understand it we shall have to describe the movements of charges that produce the "action potential," as physiologists call it. An action potential propagated from one neuron to another is what an impulse is.

As the reader already knows, electrical charges are of two kinds: positive and negative. Charges that are alike (two positive or two negative) repel one another, whereas charges that are different (one positive and one negative) attract one another. Thus, when unlike charges are separated they tend to come together; a measurement of the force that occurs is called a "potential difference." Physiologists tell us that both the cytoplasm of neurons and the extracellular fluid that bathes the neurons contain a number of ions--charged particles--in solution that attract and repel one another. The principal ions involved in the action potential are sodium and potassium, so a description of what they do when a neuron is excited will reveal the essential character of the impulse.

The main carrier of the impulse is the nerve axon, which is an extension, usually more or less elongated, of the cell body. The axon is bounded by a membrane, on both sides of which are ions in solution. As is commonly known, whenever particles are more concentrated in one part of a solution than in another, they will diffuse throughout the solution so as to equalize their distribution. The diffusion can take place through a membrane provided it is permeable. The membrane of the nerve axon has openings called "channels" that make it permeable to both sodium and potassium ions. Furthermore, the membrane can open and close its channels so that at one moment it is not very permeable to sodium ions and at another it is much more so. The same can be said about the membrane in regard to potassium ions.

In a resting, unexcited, neuron the membrane is more permeable to potassium ions than it is to sodium ions; and as a consequence potassium ions diffuse out of the cell, thereby bringing about a net charge difference, with more positive ions outside the cell and more negative (chloride) ions inside the cell. But though the membrane of the resting cell is more permeable to potassium than to sodium ions, some of the latter do diffuse into the cell. An equilibrium in the exchange of ions is -70 millivolts, the net negative charge being located inside. In this state the membrane is said to be "hyperpolarized."

When a neuron is stimulated, the permeability of its membrane is changed so that the channels which pass sodium ions are opened, resulting in a greatly increased diffusion of sodium ions into the cell, also resulting in the inside of the cell becoming positive and the outside negative. In such a condition the membrane is said to be "depolarized," and depolarization is the central event of the action potential.

When the outside of the membrane becomes the locus of a net negative charge, positive charges farther along on the membrane move toward the region of negative charge; and correspondingly, when the inside of the membrane becomes the locus of a net positive charge, negative charges on the inside of the membrane move towards the region that is positive. As a consequence of these subsequent movements the permeability of the membrane in the area from which the farther ions move becomes altered, so that at this second point on the membrane sodium ions now begin to diffuse rapidly into the cell, thereby depolarizing a second area of the membrane and setting up an action potential at that site. The process continues in this way, the action potential traveling the length of the axon in a wave-like manner. After depolarization the depolarized membranes are restored to a hyperpolarized state by sodium-potassium pumps that move sodium ions out of the cell and potassium ions into it, thereby making the membrane once more ready to undergo an action potential.

Although action potentials show "spikes" corresponding to the alternating states of depolarization and hyperpolarization, the amplitude of the action potential is constant. Their frequencies vary, however, as well as their speed along membranes of different sizes.

Now the description above admittedly lacks details, but it is adequate for the issues we are treating here and permits us to ask

the important question: is sensation sufficiently described when
we say that it is an action potential on the membranes of neurons?
or is something essential left out?   Does the description illumine,
does it satisfactorily explain what we know from ordinary
experience? does it define sensation as the identity theory would
require?
     As a first step in our reply to these questions, let us look at the
words of physiologists themselves:

> Although the electricity produced by living cells is
> often referred to as bioelectricity, it is no different
> from any other type of electricity since it results from
> charge separation and movement. The mechanisms
> living cells use to produce electricity are simple in
> principle and by no means unique to living tissues.[2]

The authors' claim that the electricity of cells is no different from
any other electricity is plainly correct. Electric currents do not
differ intrinsically just because some occur in copper wires, others
in aluminum, others in solutions, etc. And although an impulse is
not the same thing as a current in a wire, nonetheless, electrical
charge separation in cells is essentially the same as electrical
charge separation in other stuffs, and the statement the
physiologists made must be recognized as correct. But that raises a
difficulty; and in order to appreciate it more fully, we shall
examine an argument that has been presented in another kind of
subject matter.
     Writing about rebellious students of the sixties, Kenneth
Keniston criticizes an explanation some theorists had offered in
order to account for their rebellious activities. Neither the
students of an earlier nor those of a later day showed the same
rebellious spirit, and to explain its presence in students of the
sixties, some psychoanalysts had proposed what Keniston calls the
"Oedipal Rebellion theory." This account proposes that blind,
Oedipal hatred of fathers and the older generation was responsible
for the student revolts. Keniston, however, finds the explanation
insufficient on the following grounds:

There are two basic problems with Oedipal Rebellion
theory, however.   First, although it uses psychoanalytic terms, it is bad psychoanalysis.   The real
psychoanalytic account insists that the Oedipus
complex is universal in all normally developing
children.   To point to this complex in explaining
student rebellion is, therefore, like pointing to the
fact that all children learn to walk.   Since both
characteristics are said to be universal, neither helps
us understand why, at some historical moments,
students are restive and rebellious, while at others
they are not.   Second, the theory does not help us
explain why some students (especially those from
middle class, affluent and idealist families) are most
inclined to rebel, while others (especially those from
working class and deprived families) are less so.[3]

The Oedipal Rebellion theory is a bad explanation because the
Oedipus complex is present in all children, those who revolt as well
as those who do not.   In short, *because the Oedipus complex is
common to all the members of the human species, it cannot be the
cause of behavior that is proper to a subgroup.*
    The kind of objection that tells against the Oedipal Rebellion
theory also tells against the claim that sensation is a physiological
process, that sensation is an impulse.   Because the latter is
essentially the propagation along a membrane of a potential
difference that results from an initial separation of charges and
their subsequent motions, the electrical pulse is a property which
cannot explain behavior that is less common than the electrical
property itself.   That it is less common is certainly the case, for
"sensation" is taken to signify something that occurs only in
certain organisms, not in all living things, much less the
inanimate.   But if someone still insists that the electrical activities
are the sensation, then he has to say that sensation occurs *wherever
they occur*, whether in neural tissue, muscle tissue, or laboratory
solutions containing charges separated by a permeable membrane.
    But if someone argues that an electrical pulse is sufficient to
define sensation because it is in the brain, because it is in neurons,
which are in some ways different from other cells as well as from
inanimate materials, then his argument surreptitiously introduces

a hidden difference. Although nerve tissue is indeed different from other tissues, *the nature of the electrical phenomenon is not.* Hence by pointing to the special character of neurons, an appeal actually is being made to *an unseen difference in the tissue itself.* And granted that sensation is limited to some organisms, the unseen difference would actually be responsible for what is distinct in sensation. The electrical property would then be employed in the explanation as a kind of false cause, or else as a generic attribute, the undescribed difference in the tissue being the hidden but "true" cause.

The unreasonableness of the position becomes more apparent if we consider again the relation of a property to its subjects. One electrical current does not differ from another because one is in copper and the other in silver or aluminum, etc. Nor does heat itself become different when it occurs in more than one kind of stuff. Despite differences in metals the cause responsible for the electricity is the same in each, and despite differences in stuffs the cause of their being hot is also the same in each. And so it is with other activities or properties. Thus we see that since a potential difference is caused by charge separation, the fact that the subject is brain tissue in one case, muscle tissue in another, or a solution in a laboratory container separated into parts by a membrane in still another, is irrelevant to the nature of the potential difference and its coming and going. In short, the *process* is the same whether it is in the brain or elsewhere.

The point we have made is confirmed by a remark of Ragnar Granit, a Nobel laureate:

> Impulses . . . are alike *in all sensory nerve fibers* (emphasis ours) and their genesis is reasonably well understood in physicochemical terms, yet this knowledge does not help us very much to understand their different effects on the senses.[4]

We all know that the sensation of blue and the sensation of red are not the same; neither are the sensation of red and the sensation of hearing middle C. Yet as Granit says, "impulses are alike in all sensory nerve fibers." So in effect he employs in a more particular way the same argument we introduced above. But there is another application of the argument that is still more particular. When we simultaneously *see* the color and the shape of a tennis ball, we have only one impulse in our sense of sight. How, then, does the one action potential distinguish between the traits? (Even if there were two potentials, how could they be distinguished?) And so it would seem that we must examine sensation on other grounds.

C. Sensation: its own characteristics

According to *Webster's Third International* dictionary, "sensation" signifies

> a state of consciousness produced by impingement of
> an external object or condition upon the body; . . . a
> mode of mental cognitive functioning referable to
> immediate stimulation of the body from without.

Taking the most general categories we can get from these listings, sensation is considered to be either a state (internal) or a function. If we then ask what *Webster's* says about function, we find the following:

> . . . the action for which a person or thing is
> specifically fitted, used, or responsible or for which a
> thing exists: the activity appropriate to the nature or
> position of a person or thing.

Ordinary experience classifies sensation as a *function* (this word is equivocal as said of natural and artefactual entities, and we are here speaking of those that are natural) which is an *action* or an activity; so because a sensation can be said to be either a state or an action, it can be looked at under two aspects. First, a sensation actually does give a determination to the subject in which it is found, for there is a real difference between the conditions of sensing and non-sensing. We speak of a state as a state *of something*, and in so doing we call attention to it as a property of the subject in which it occurs. "Action" and "activity," however, bring to mind something else to which the action or activity is directed, namely, its object; and this is the point of importance.

The actions which are most obvious to us are those that are physical and have observable results; or in other words, those activities which are physical and have observable results are the first the mind knows. We cut and plane boards, heat water, mold clay, plough the ground, mix cement, paint walls, bend pipes, throw and hit balls, etc. And nature is responsible for similar doings: the sun warms the earth, the wind blows seeds, glaciers move boulders, waves erode shores, the moon raises tides, celestial bodies attract one another, etc. In all of these there is both an agent that acts and *something toward which the act is directed*, that is, an object in which the agent brings about a real modification; and that is what the word "action" first signifies. Were the sun the only body in existence, it would do no heating even though it would possess all that it needed in order to heat. The sun would be hot but not heating. More generally, these actions are founded on relations between active and passive physical qualities.

In an important way, however, sensation stands in contrast to the activities listed above, because from the point of view of public, external experience, the activity of sensation itself is unobservable and does not have observable results. The movements of eyeballs, fingers, etc., although necessary, are not the sensations themselves; much less so are the bodily movements that are signs of internal affective states.[5] Yet despite their difference, physical and sensory activity do resemble one another to some extent, for we know from our experience of eliciting and controlling our sensory operations that they require both an organism that does the sensing and *an object toward which the sensing is directed*. Moreover, a property of the object is that of which we are first aware when we sense; we are first aware of a reality external to us.[6] But as we said a moment ago, unlike physical activities, our looking at something--the moon, for instance--*does not modify what we look at, nor does anything happen to the piano when we listen to the sounds it gives forth*. Even when we feel warmth or wetness or softness or heaviness in something, the touching sensation itself does not modify the object that is felt; and this is what we meant when we said that sensation does not have observable results.[7] Although a physical contact (and hence a physical modification) is necessary for a tactile sensation, the contact is not the operation.

In short, there is a radical difference between physical and sensory activity, a point we must develop.

Sensation can be called an activity; yet because it does not modify the object toward which it is directed, *it cannot be categorized with the activities that do modify their objects*, which means that the word "activity" is equivocal and has an extended sense when it is applied to sensation. Moreover, because sensation does not modify its object its "role" is to "add" a determination to the subject, the organism, in which it occurs, and this accounts for our calling the function a "state." An organism that senses has advantages an organism which does not sense cannot have. On the other hand, the action of heating and any other like it "adds" a determination not to the body that does the heating but to the body that is heated, as is plain when the sun heats the land or the sea. Our statement is true even when a movement of some part of the agent is necessary to affect the object, as for instance, sawing, cutting, or hitting. The movements of limbs are not by themselves an advantage to the agent, although they are necessary for and presupposed to the modification of the object. (To be sure, the modification of the object can be and is intended ultimately to be advantageous to the agent.) In sum, then, the two kinds of activity are irreducibly distinct and must be classified in different basic categories. But let us make use of the distinction.

An impulse is a modification that moves along a train of neurons. It is initiated by a stimulus and is similar to an electric current that moves along a wire or to water that flows in a pipe. In these latter two cases, one part of the wire or one part of the water affects another successively. Similarly, as a result of being stimulated, the carrier-subject's parts are modified in a direction that is away from the stimulating agent and towards the receiver. On the other hand, a sensory function as such is an operation through which we are aware of a reality distinct from us, and it is in a "direction" that is away from us towards the stimulus, which would seem to argue that it cannot be solely an electrical pulse.

Many have noted other attributes we assign to sensation-- seeing, for instance--that serve to make the differences between the kinds of activity more determinate. First, a visual impulse travels along the optic nerve, whereas seeing cannot be said to travel along the nerve, for it is thought to occur in the visual cortex. Second, an impulse has a velocity, and so could be faster or slower; but we would never allow that we could see faster or slower. Third, an impulse has a frequency; it is a current that oscillates, but seeing does not oscillate. We must add that assigning such attributes does not beg the question; for we are aware of their absence by the same internal experience that shows us that there is such a thing as sensation. In short, the physiological process has attributes that we cannot assign to the sensation. Assertions to the contrary will come only from those who assume as their starting point that which is contested, namely, that sensations are identical to impulses propagated along membranes.

D. Essentials recapitulated

Objections to identity theories are the following:

1) The "morning star" theory names one thing from two properties: but an identity of subject does not establish identity of the properties named.
2) Reductionism identifies the property with the parts of the subject that are the cause of the property.
3) *Sensation* and *brain process* cannot be formally identical:
    a) because charge separation and movement are found where sensation is not;
    b) because the electrical phenomenon itself is not differentiated by different subjects;
    c) because the impulse has properties sensation does not have.

Notes to Chapter 15

[1]The physiological description that follows is taken from Arthur J. Vander, James H. Sherman, Dorothy S. Luciano, *Human Physiology*, 2nd ed. (New York: McGraw-Hill,Inc., 1975), Ch. 6; and *Scientific American*, September, 1979. This entire issue of *Scientific American* is on the brain. See especially, "The Neuron," by Charles S. Stevens. Use has been made also of a longer work:

John C. Eccles, *The Understanding of the Brain* (New York: McGraw-Hill Book Company, 1973).

[2]Arthur J. Vander, 1st ed., 1970, p. 123.

[3]"How the New Generation Got that Way," in *Philosophy for a New Generation*, A. K. Bierman, James A. Gould, eds. (New York: The Macmillan Company, 1970).

[4]Ragnar Granit, *The Purposive Brain* (Cambridge, Massachusetts: The MIT Press, 1977), p. 21.

[5]It is important to keep these many things distinct. A sensation of seeing red (as in blood) is not the same as the emotional response that may follow on the sensation. Nor are internal states to be confused with or even necessarily related to the physical movements of the body, from slight muscle tremors to blushing, etc., that can accompany internal states.

[6]The point has been made at length that young children are not aware of their own internal acts of thinking as distinct from the objects known. They make the distinction only later. See Jean Piaget, *The Child's Conception of the World* (Totowa, New Jersey: Littlefield, Adams & Co., 1965), ch. 1.

[7]Our mode of speaking about sensation resembles the mode we use in talking about physical activity. When the sun heats, the sea is being heated, it is heated. The change in temperature at issue is one and the same in each case. "Heats" signifies the change insofar as it is brought about by the sun, which is the agent. "Is being heated" or "is heated" signifies the change in temperature insofar as the latter is a modification received by the subject. And when we see, we say that the mountain is "being seen" or "is seen" or "is looked at"; and here the mode of speaking but not the reality is the same as that employed to talk about the object that is heated. The expression is properly called an "extrinsic denomination," and such expressions cannot be avoided because acts of sensation do have objects that they attain, though they do not modify the objects.

CHAPTER 16

SENSATION: OBJECTIONS
AND ELABORATIONS

A. Some objections

Having presented the essential elements of our position, we would now like to consider a few objections taken from Levin, one of which is farther removed from the central issue and will be dealt with first.

Levin seeks to upset opponents who attack the materialist identification of mental acts and brain states with the claim

> that among the properties of brain states are spatial properties that cannot be assigned to mental states. It is said, for example, that thoughts have no spatial location; since brain processes do, the two cannot be identical.[1]

Levin regards this objection as

> fallacious. Processes have no spatial location; so thoughts need have none even if they are brain processes. Objects are what have spatial location. It

is nerve cells, not brain processes or states, that have
locations. A process *can* be assigned the location of
its constituents but this is an extension of the word
'location' as it is used when denied application to
thoughts.[2]

Let us say at once that formally speaking we think Levin is right.
No property has a location in the strict sense of the term; location is
itself a property of the thing. On the other hand, Levin does
concede that in an extended sense properties can be said to be
located insofar as they belong to an "object" that is located. And as
we know, seeing occurs on the visual cortex, a pain is in a finger,
etc. It seems, therefore, that the materialist position has to be
sustained in regard to locating some mental acts. Perhaps there is
more ground for suspecting that thinking--the mental in the fullest
sense of the term--may not be located the way seeing or a pain is;
yet even if this position is to be asserted it must be proved.
Certainly it cannot be taken as a starting point for non-materialist
claims.

Levin's concession, however, is important. If, for example, we
were to heat one end of an iron rod, we would say that heat is
transferred along the rod until the last part is affected and all
sections of the rod have undergone a rise in temperature. In
making such a statement, not only do we assign a location to the
heating but a direction as well. We use an expression that implies
direction, "heat is transferred", because ordinary experience
justifies our saying that one part of the rod affects another that is
adjacent to it. The same is true when the rod conducts an electric
current or when it transmits sounds along some dimension. Even
mechanical motion--for instance,when one end of a rod is pushed
the whole is moved--is to be regarded as located and directed in a
similar way. And who will deny that an alternating current is
located in a conductor and that it reverses direction? But our point
is this: if properties are located by reason of the parts or subjects
they are in, then so are modifications of those properties.

None of these remarks are news, but they do have an
application to the issue; for an impulse is propagated from one part
of an axon to another and from one neuron to another and so passes
from one location to another in a determinate direction. Can we
say, however, that seeing or hearing is propagated from one part of

an axon to another, that it travels and has a direction? Since we are aware of our sensations, we ought also to be aware of their moving from one location to another. Thus it would seem that although this kind of location and direction does belong to brain processes, it does not belong to sensations.

There is another point that can be drawn out from a statement Levin makes about the mental act of noticing:

> The materialist holds that noticing a lemon is a brain
> state, in some causal relation to a lemon.[3]

As he says, the act of noticing a lemon bears a causal relation to a lemon; the state of the one sensing is related to the external object that is sensed. On that account brain states imply relations to other things, and so we must examine the character of this causal relation, at least in a minimal way.

There is no doubting that a sensation depends upon a property of some thing that acts as a stimulus. But to say that something is a stimulus is to say that it is active and that it modifies something else which is passive. The physiologist, of course, seeks to explain this modification; he seeks to explain how neurons undergo action potentials as a consequence of an activity by a stimulus. But once again we should note that insofar as an action potential depends on a stimulus, *neural tissue is passive*. Neural tissue is affected by, but it does not in turn affect the stimulus. The impulse does not modify the stimulating object, and in this respect the sensory apparatus is related to the stimulus in the same way the sea is related to the sun that heats it. Just as the activity of heating is "from the sun to the sea," so in neural tissue the activity is "from the stimulus to the sensory apparatus." *On a physiological* level there is no active relation of any kind the other way around.

But we do know through actually seeing and hearing that there is something is us by which we are related to the object in the "reverse direction"; that is, we are active in respect to the sensed reality despite our not effecting a modification in it. Formally taken, sensation is "from us to the exterior object" at which it terminates. And though we have said these things before, we need now to look at another way in which the passivity of the sense can be considered.

All are aware that we initiate and direct the application of the sensory operation. Because we can choose to look or not to look at something, we are active in that regard; yet we do not determine *what* we see, *what kind* of sensory response we have. Whether we see red or green, whether we hear high or low C, depends on the objects sensed, which makes us passive in regard to their specifying activity. Thus because we direct the application of our senses, because we strive to hear sounds, etc., we are active. But since what we sense is determined by the object we are also passive, and this is the way the object stands in a causal relation to sensation proper. This dual character is not found in any of the physical operations according to which inanimate stuffs are affected. The qualities which make such activities possible are specified prior to the action and do not depend on something coming from the object.

B. Pleasure and pain

Before we leave the mind-body problem, a few words about pleasure and pain. Uncontestably there is a non-fictional difference between the man who suffers pain upon sensing an object and the same man when he does not suffer such pain. We are all aware that pleasures and pains are realities that exist as modifications of a substance; that is, that they are transient properties. The character of each, however, is not adequately described as long as we do not know what is special about them; so let us note some remarks of a biologist:

> The pleasures derived from eating, for instance, serve a profound purpose. Physiologists once used to judge the value of goods by their calorie contents alone. Each gram of fat, albumin, or carbohydrate that you introduce into your stomach gives you a certain amount of physical energy that can be expressed in units of heat, as so many calories. Your body needs this energy as a steam engine needs the energy supplied by coal. But if your cook served you merely a mixture of these substances, even though they are very important per se, you would be highly indignant. The taste of the food has absolutely

nothing to do with these sources of energy; flavor is the product of all sorts of admixtures of other substances that although they lack all calorie content, perform an important duty in whetting the appetite. Appetite not only makes the eater "dig into his food" more enthusiastically than he could without it, but aids the proper functioning of his intestinal canal.[4]

The author goes on to expand upon these remarks, and then he turns his attention to pain:

While pleasurable sensations are the most powerful motives that make human beings and animals perform biologically important acts, the unpleasurable ones are designed by Nature to deter unreasoning creatures from doing things that could result in harm to them. We are acquainted with a great many such sensations within our sensory world; loathing, pain, and bitter tastes are but a few. Their presence serves a purpose similar to that of pleasant sensations.[5]

Both pleasure and pain, we hear, are biologically functional.[6] Pleasure inclines an animal to act in pursuit of something; pain inclines it to act by avoiding something. Like external sensations, pleasure and pain are both states that imply a relation of an animal to something in its habitat or environment. Pain regularly--if not always--indicates a disproportion between the animal and the object which produces the pain, whereas pleasure regularly indicates a proportion. Pleasurable objects are proportioned to an activity an animal can perform on them or in regard to them, and the pleasurable objects are regularly beneficial to the animal or to its species or both. Pain on the other hand, indicates to the animal that it must avoid something damaging. Because a particular object can be proportioned or disproportioned to one animal and not to another, it causes pleasure or pain in one but not in the other. Thus pleasure and pain *imply relations to the object over and above the properties which might initially describe the object*; and however inaccessible pleasure and pain may be to external observation and however obscure their natures, we nevertheless can know something essential about them. We know they are functions of bodily parts and tissues, and we also know they are principles of actions. Pleasure and pain incline animals to pursue or to avoid something; so they cannot be states that are purely passive and in no way active. In sum, pleasure and pain also involve more than the electrical activities that define *brain process*.

C. Intelligence and the human species

We know that sensation cannot be reduced to electrical activities, so on that account sentient organisms constitute a class of material substance. But we may also note that one more division in substances can be established: man is a species that is distinct from all others. Here again an operation is the key, for only man can think in the strict sense of the word; that is, only man can draw conclusions from premises, infer theorems from axioms. Some people like to define intelligence as a "problem solving capacity," and if we take that description as our measure, we see that the expression is equivocal. Man, but not other organisms, solves problems in quantum mechanics, chemistry, tensor calculus, philosophy, history, linguistics, etc., which means that when we consider that which is most obviously human, we find no evidence of any kind to warrant our saying that what is characteristically human can be found in any other primate, much less in inferior organisms. But we shall not labor the point. At the least, we can say that thinking in a strict sense does not occur in all animals, which means that humans form another class of substances distinguished by their own kind of behavioral capacity. If, however, it should turn out that some other primate truly can think in the sense in which we do, then we shall have to grant him all the socio-political rights and privileges that follow therefrom.

D. Epilogue

To close this chapter, we think it relevant to note how strongly men are inclined to favor scientific theories over ordinary experience, that is, over empirical regularities open to ordinary observation. Our habits of mind are so strong that sometimes we altogether overlook or ignore the obvious in favor of what someone has taught us or in favor of "what is being said." If one asks an undergraduate student what light is, very likely the answer he hears will tell about photons that travel at 300,000 kilometers per second, etc.; the student does not begin with what ordinary experience reveals.

Yet when we explicitly ask what ordinary observation shows about light, we note that some bodies--for instance the sun or a hot iron bar--are visible by reason of a property in them. We say they are "luminescent," and if they are bright enough we call them "lights." Other bodies, however, are not visible in that way but become visible only in the presence of something luminescent, a light. This second kind of body may be colored or transparent, but the visibility it has is dependent on the luminescent body. Such are the data of ordinary experience.

Although our scientific theories go beyond such data, they do depend on it. Theory tells us, for instance, that light travels and is propagated as photons; yet if we ask "How do we know that light travels?" we refer to observations made of a celestial body that is delayed in its predicted appearance. A traveling visible body is calculated to appear at a certain time at a point in the heavens, but it does not; it appears later. To explain the delay, we assume that light travels. We take into account the length of the delay together with the distance the visible body is from us, and we then calculate the speed at which light travels. Hence the beginning of our understanding of light as a thing traveling is our ordinary experience; and all theories begin the same way, whether they seek to account for electromagnetic radiation or gravitational attraction or sensation. (Observing the macroscopic body might require a simple telescope, but that hardly puts the observation beyond the realm of ordinary experience, any more than the use of a magnifying glass to see a fingerprint.)

But there is a more important point to consider. To say that light consists of photons does nothing at all to explain why we can see the sun 93 million miles away. How do photons that strike our retinas here on earth enable us to see something very far away? We have to start our considerations by accepting the reality of the distant object, yet neither waves nor energy quanta tell us why we can attain it. Similarly, gravitons that are emitted by the earth and strike the moon do nothing at all to explain why the moon is attracted toward the earth. However useful gravitons may be for certain theoretical considerations and however real they may be, by themselves they are no more a complete account of gravitational motion than photons are of seeing distant objects. And so it should not be surprising that accounts of sensation that are given in terms of electrical theories are even more deficient and incomplete as explanations of sensation than photons and gravitons are of electromagnetic radiation and gravitation. We are very certain that we do elicit sensory activities which in a real but mysterious way put us in touch with objects in the world outside us.

To finish, I would like to quote a remark Brand Blanshard once made:

> Now this view that an ache or a pain is nothing but a change in bodily tissue is silly. There would not be the least absurdity, although no doubt there are difficulties, in saying that the pain is caused by a physical change or that the two are differing manifestations of something that lies behind them; but to say that it is the pain is to say what no one can really think and what only a thoroughly muddled head could suppose he thought. If a great many otherwise sensible people do suppose that they think it, this can only be because they have confused it with some other theory of a similar sound, such as that there is an extremely close dependence of mind on body. But unfortunately, as Paulsen has pointed out, 'the absurd has this advantage in common with truth, that it cannot be refuted.'[7]

Although some of his words are harsh, Blanshard makes a sound point; and even Nagel, as explicit as he is, might not fully see the difference between identity and "an extremely close dependence."

Notes to Chapter 16

[1]Op. cit., p. 100.

[2]Ibid.

[3]Ibid., p. 97.

[4]Wolfgang Von Buddenbrock, *The Senses* (Ann Arbor, Michigan: The University of Michigan Press, 1956), p. 46.

[5]Ibid., p. 49.

[6]It is plain that both we and von Buddenbrock are speaking of that pain which arises from the sensations of external objects. The pain which results from disease or malfunction serves a similar purpose however; it tells us to avoid the use of the injured part.

[7]"The Nature of Thought" (London: George Allen and Unwin, Ltd., 1939). Reprinted in *Metaphysics*, Julius R. Weinberg, Keith E. Yandell, eds. (New York: Holt, Rinehart and Winton, Inc.).

CHAPTER 17

A FINAL ARGUMENT

A. Disappearing properties

Minerals, which are solids, have various crystalline shapes, geologists tell us, that follow upon their molecular structures. Liquids, on the other hand, have no fixed shape. Ordinarily they take on the forms of their containers, except that in drops or droplets they spontaneously become spherical; and the spherical shape is the result of surface tension forces that are found in fluids. But cells are fluid-like, viscous substances; so we might well expect them--particularly unicellular organisms--to be spherical. (Especially ought this to be the case, it would seem, if cells are simply arrangements of compounds.) But let us listen to a biologist:

> When we remember that *protoplasm* (the name applied to all the living contents of a cell) is a viscous substance bounded by a semi-elastic outer membrane, we naturally assume that the shape of these cells would be spherical, since their surface tension, particularly in those that are free-floating, should form them in the same way that surface tension shapes airborne soap bubbles and rubber balloons. Many cells, indeed, do have a spherical structure:

the eggs of many marine animals when released into
water, many yeasts and bacteria, and a variety of
unicellular algae. But from the different shapes
attained by other forms of unicellular life, it appears
certain that the organism itself rather than surface
tension or external forces exerts a dominant effect on
its shape. Some bacteria are rods, spirals, and even
commas; among the algae, the diatoms, desmids, and
dinoflagellates, with their unusual contours and
outer skeletons, take on a bizarre appearance. Even
the amoeba, familiar to most of you, is not normally a
sphere. Generally flattened because it rests on a
surface, it has no particular shape, but rather is a
fluid blob of protoplasm that can flow this way or
that; only at rest or in death does it round up.[1]

As far as their external form is concerned, cells do not behave
according to the physical laws for viscous stuffs, and as a
consequence the author of the passage above concludes that the
"organism itself" is determinative of the cell's shape. To make
plain what he means, he goes on in subsequent passages to describe
how cell shapes are adapted to cell functions, making them more
efficient:

When we turn to a consideration of the cell shapes of
multicellular organisms, we find that mechanical
forces still determine form to some extent, but that
the function a cell performs is also a factor in the
shaping process. . . .

The human red blood cell is spherical when viewed
face on, flattened and concave when seen from the
side. Its function, of course, is to transport oxygen
from the lungs to the tissues and carbon dioxide from
the tissues to the lungs. Its thin dimensions permit it
to exchange gases rapidly, while its rounded contours
allow it to slide easily through even the smallest
capillaries. A spherical cell would be useless in this
respect, for the gas exchange between the exterior of

> the cell and its center would be very slow in
> proportion to its size. . . .
>
> [Muscle cells] contract violently when a muscle is in
> action, while [nerve cells], which may reach over
> three feet in length in a human, are part of an
> extensive communication network--the telephone
> system, if you will--for relaying messages throughout
> the body. Imagine, if you can, a nerve or muscle cell
> having a spherical or flat shape. Would it be able to
> perform its function as efficiently?[2]

Although mechanical forces play their role, *function has the last word in determining cell shape*, and with that in mind, let us now return to something the author said earlier.

An amoeba, he told us, is ordinarily flattened in shape, and "only at rest or in death does it round up." This point is of some importance: upon its death an "amoeba" obeys the laws of physics in the sense that its shape after death is determined solely by surface tension forces; the ordinary flattened shape of the living amoeba has disappeared. From this it is plain that cell shape is a property determined by the function or operation of the living whole itself; and once the whole loses its proper functional character, it loses its characteristic shape also. In short, the disappearance of properties prepares us for considering something else, namely, the disappearance of operational capacities from parts of an organism that are removed from their wholes. Removal involves a kind of death of the part, not in every sense of the term, but a death that brings about the loss of the ability to function or operate in the proper way.

B. Disappearing operations

Seeing is not an operation that is found in molecules; instead it appears only in an organ of sight, which here will be taken to consist of two eyeballs, two optic nerves, and the relevant parts of the brain, especially the visual cortex. (We shall speak of all this as "the eye.") Eyes, however, are unlike the parts of aggregates, particularly those of machines, because eyes cannot be separated from their wholes and still retain their operational capacities. We all know that removing the eye makes us blind. This fact of experience makes it evident that the operation of seeing properly belongs to the whole as that which sees, whereas the part--the eye-- is that by which or through which the whole sees. So because *we* see by means of a part, we may infer that the separated eye does not see. The operation of seeing is not observable by the external senses, which means that we cannot tell by examining the part that it has no act of seeing. True, the tissues of the eye might well be kept metabolically alive, an impulse might be artificially produced, and the whole eye in principle might even be transplanted to another person where it would recover its operation and enable that other person to see. Yet we do have to say that separated from the whole the eye does not see.[3]

We can make the same general point in another way, for the surgery required to separate the part from the whole would cause *you* or *me* pain; what is left of the whole would suffer, not the severed part. Moreover, attributing pain to the severed part would make it a "self," and put it on an equal footing with the damaged whole.

But if for the sake of argument we assume that the separated eye does see, then we are faced with difficulties; for we cannot explain how we, the remaining body dispossessed of sight, actually do see when the eye is still in the whole. If the separated eye is that which sees, then how do we, what is left, come to see by means of it when the eye is still in the whole? Furthermore, if the eye is properly *that which sees* rather than *that by which or through which the whole sees*, then consistency requires us to say the same for the other organs: the ear is that which hears, the nose is that which smells, etc., and we end up with a connected series of independent operational units, independent entities, each of which has its own proper activity, and none of which can communicate its operation to the others. We would truly be operational aggregates, and we would find ourselves at a loss to say how the whole can be said to perform any operation, except in an extended and improper sense. That, however, is not what an organism is; and so it would seem we must concede that the eye lost its operation when it was separated from the whole.

In contrast, a mechanical aggregate is not like an animal organism. For instance, an engine does not lose its ability to run if it is taken out of the car; a battery does not lose its capacity to produce a current; a thermostat in a heating system does not lose its ability to close and open its contacts as a result of thermal expansion and contraction. Furthermore, each of these parts is manufactured separately and endowed with its operational power *before* it is assembled in the whole. Imagine the difficulties an engineer would face if the parts of the machine were to acquire new properties and capacities as a consequence of being assembled in the whole. Successful design presupposes that such events will not come about.

Because the different natures of machines and organisms can be seen in the way each is produced, we shall note the difference that is salient. Machines are produced by a process in which each operational part is first manufactured and then all are assembled together, *whereas an organism is produced by a generative process in which the parts come into existence within the whole as it, the whole, is being produced.* The organs, the tissues, the cells, and the protein structural molecules proper to the parts are all "made to order." The parts are *not* first built and then assembled. Unlike machines, the whole and the parts of organisms are produced simultaneously. At first the whole organism has an indeterminate character; but then it develops, which means that differentiation of parts proceeds from within the whole itself. It develops itself, so to speak, and this sort of activity does not occur in machines or in aggregates of any kind.

And so to sum up. If the eye and other parts of an organism were that which acted, then a seeing animal would be like a machine, and the parts would retain their function outside the whole (assuming the parts were sustained), as well as acquire them before becoming parts of the whole. Furthermore, the parts of a machine are first produced and then assembled, whereas the whole organism exists from the start in an indeterminate way and develops its parts from within by a process of differentiation.

Before we finish this chapter we would like to quote a passage from the biologist E. S. Russell, who says in one of his books:[4]

> Through blind unconscious activities, which are orderly, co-ordinated, and directive towards specific ends, there is built up a functional organisation which is far more complex and perfect, both in its structure and its working, than anything man can

construct with the aid of his highest powers of
intelligence and manipulative ability. Directive and
creative activity without foreknowledge of the end
achieves far more striking results than the
consciously purposive action of man, and by methods
entirely different from those which he employs in
making machines, or houses. Man makes the parts of
his constructs separately and fits them together. The
egg works from within outwards; it proceeds by
growth and self-differentiation, based upon directive
metabolic activity, taking from the outside only raw
materials which it builds into its own substance;
there is no fitting together of pre-fabricated parts.
The more one considers the living organism and the
manner of its development, the less machine-like
does it appear.

With that we shall leave this topic and turn our attention to
another matter, namely, to the relation that obtains between the
superior operations, such as reproduction and sensation, and the
chemical and physical movements that are subordinate to but
necessary for those that are superior.

Notes to Chapter 17

[1]Carl P. Swanson, *The Cell* (Englewood Cliffs, New Jersey:
Prentice-Hall, Inc.,1960), pp. 13-16.

[2]Ibid.

[3]We have selected *seeing* very deliberately; not only because we
discussed it in the preceding chapter, but also because it has no
"look-alike" in machines. The movement of an animal body by
means of limbs is mechanical in character, even though it is

brought about by living tissues; the limbs are levers. But photoelectric cells do not see, and neither do cameras.

[4]*The Directiveness of Organic Activities* (Cambridge: At the University Press, 1943), pp. 172-3.

CHAPTER 18

RELATIONS AMONG ACTIVITIES

A. The question

Those who subscribe to dualism also frequently subscribe to "interactionism," which claims that the mental acts on the physical and the physical on the mental. This is taken to mean that each can act on the other "equally," in the sense that something substantively mental acts on the physical and something substantively physical acts on the mental. As we might expect, objections are raised to interactionism, one of which is based on the law of the conservation of energy. It argues that if the physical were to act on the spiritual, then the physical would have to expend energy, and energy expended on a spiritual substance would disappear from the physical universe and would seem to be annihilated, in violation of the first law of thermodynamics. But apart from this and other objections, interactionism is inadmissible on the grounds that it requires an aggregate composed of distinct material and immaterial substances; and difficulties such as the one above stem from that implicit assumption. On the other hand, we do generally concede that the mental and the physical *in some way* affect each other, to which psychosomatic medicine as well as ordinary human experience testify. Hence the question arises as to how this happens. We shall begin our answer by drawing attention to the starting points we shall employ.

First, let us admit that interactionism in the usual sense (we shall leave room for an extended sense) is inadmissible. Second, let us recall that organisms have operations not found in inanimate substances. Third, let us also recall that physical movements and chemical reactions do indeed occur in things which maintain themselves, grow, and reproduce. So in the light of these propositions the question becomes: what is the relation between the operations that characterize the non-living and those that are proper to the living as such? Taking sensation as an example, if an impulse is not an act of seeing, then what is its relation to that activity? At the least it has something to do with sensation and stands in some causal relation to it. Stated in a general form, the question would seem to be: what is the relation of physical and chemical activities to the peculiarly biological activities of an organism?

B. Instances of inanimate activities in organisms

That within organisms there are the kinds of physical and chemical processes characteristic of the inanimate is beyond dispute; cell division itself shows their existence. For example, the dividing process requires spindle fibers constructed for the purpose of pulling apart pairs of chromosomes, which is a physical movement, and it also requires analytic and synthetic chemical activities for the dissolution and reconstitution of ribosomes. To aid growth, there is osmotic flow through cell membranes, diffusion within the cell, etc. In larger organisms, mechanical expansion and contraction moves air in and out of lungs, and mechanical pumping circulates blood. But our point is simply that the general kinds of physical movements and chemical processes which characterize the inanimate also occur in organisms, without which the operations proper to organisms could not occur. Thus, we are brought back to the question: what is the nature of the relation between physical and chemical activities on the one hand and peculiarly biological operations on the other? The first step on the way to an answer will be to examine some ordinary things that can throw light on the issue.

C. Instruments

Tools and utensils are made for specific functions; that is to say, the materials and design give rise to a distinct functional capacity. Knives slice, screwdrivers turn screws, hammers drive nails, pliers grip things, etc. Functions, of course, are the usual means for determining the character of the instrument, which is to say that the function and constitution go together. From the point of view of actual existence and the exercise of function, the nature of the tool or utensil determines the character of the function. Knives and chisels, for instance, although they are passive and have to be applied to objects by men, are designed for cutting or slicing activities, and slicing results in one part of a stuff being separated from another.

But knives and chisels are used by sculptors to carve statues, and when we compare these tools to the production of a statue of Socrates, say, we see that the they are not sufficient by themselves to bring about the result. Yet in the hands of sculptors, tools serve to produce effects that exceed the capacities of the tools themselves. The sculptor acts as the principal agent, the principal active cause, while the tool acts as *an instrumental agent or cause*; yet it does stand in a real causal relation to the effect. A tool "produces" only in a diminished sense, and its own proper action is elevated by the principal agent. But because of this subordination, because a sculptor moves and directs his tools, carving a statue is a single operation in which the instrument is related to an effect beyond the instrument's own functional capacity. An instrument can exceed the limits of its own form or design because of the directed motion it receives in the hands of the sculptor. A chisel can slice off a shaving, but it cannot by itself slice an image of Socrates. And so an agent cause is rightly regarded as an instrument when it is a cause of something that exceeds its own, inherent active capacities.

We must emphasize that a tool has its own nature and function antecedently to being used by a principal agent; the latter presupposes the functional capacity of the instrument he employs. Furthermore, the tool's function actually does enter into the effect, which we readily see in the statue of Socrates. Furthermore, a defective instrument may very well result in a defective effect. This is apparent if we consider a television technician faced with the task of repairing a set. If in order to diagnose an ill he employs a signal generator to drive a signal through a circuit, and then reads the signal on an oscilloscope, he can diagnose the ill. But if the waveform on the screen is distorted by a defect in the oscilloscope itself, he will make an incorrect diagnosis and consequently an inappropriate modification of the set. In short, a defective tool can result in a defective effect.

That there are instrumental agents in nature is beyond doubt once we realize that biological operations are sui generis. For instance, if we say "Reactants (or compounds) A and B combine to form a (another) compound," we signify an effect--the compound--that is proportioned to the inherent operational capacities of the reactants. But if we say "Compounds A, B, etc. combine to form a cell," then we signify an effect which is *not* proportioned to the inherent operational capacities of the reactants. More generally, when we say that chemical reactions produce living tissues or maintain organisms or bring about their growth, we speak of the reactions in relation to effects that exceed the capacities of the compounds considered according to their own proper active capacities. Again, by themselves neither elements nor compounds can produce living entities or parts of them, for if they could, they would have additional active capacities and would not be merely compounds. Thus, the reactants are instrumental in relation to a principal active source, not insofar as the elements produce a compound, but insofar as elements or compounds produce something living.

The other activities we mentioned in section B are also instrumental: blood movement in higher organisms, respiration, bulk flow, diffusions, osmosis, etc. An article in *Scientific American*[1] provides an interesting example when it discusses the ability of barn owls to locate moving prey in complete darkness by means of hearing alone. To locate their prey accurately, owls make use of differences that occur in the propagation of sounds, such as the very small time interval between the impressions on the two ear drums, as well as phase differences that allow waves to cancel and reenforce one another. And in regard to sight, we know *that* nerve impulses are instrumental in relation to sensation, though we must concede that we do not know *how*. Moreover, sensations themselves, whether in the external apparatus or in the memory, function instrumentally in relation to the formation of propositions and arguments, which surpass images, David Hume notwithstanding. And since the senses are necessary instruments, damage to them can interfere with or inhibit altogether the processes of the intelligence. Summing up, we may say that physical movements and modifications, as well as chemical reactions, operate as instruments in relation to the principal activities of reproduction, growth, self-maintenance, and sensations of all kinds.

Instruments in nature are not confined to organisms, for they occur elsewhere too. When an ocean current brings together two atoms or molecules that react to form a compound, the transporting movement is instrumental in relation to the reaction that follows the union of the atoms or molecules. To repeat, translational motion is instrumental when it is compared to the product that results from the chemical reaction. In a similar way catalysts are instruments of reactions, since their function is also to bring atoms or molecules together.

The production of materials such as plastics shows the role men themselves play as instruments in regard to certain chemical reactions. By isolating reactants and bringing them together under conditions nature does not provide, chemical elements and compounds undergo reactions they would otherwise not, producing thereby compounds nature does not produce. Still, the actions of men are only instrumental to the natural capacities of the reactants, which are principally responsible for the reaction that takes place and the stuff it produces. That is the sense in which plastics *et alia* are man-made. They are said to be "not natural" only in an extended sense. Their principal causes, the elements, are natural in the full sense of the word.

The difference between interactionism and the position we have been defending should now be plain; for interactionism assumes that two separate, substantive entities react on one another as principal agents. But when one agent is subordinated as an instrument to another, there is no mutual, reciprocal activity between them *in a strict sense*. Instead, the principal agent moves and directs the instrument in a single unified operation, while the instrument "acts" on the principal agent insofar as its operational capacity limits and specifies what the principal agent does. This may be called "interactionism," but only in a diminished sense.

D. Natural and artefactual instruments: a comparison

Manifestly there are similarities between artefactual and natural instruments. Just as artefactual instruments are produced by human agents, so many instrumental compounds are produced by organisms themselves. And just as the human agent moves and directs his instruments to an effect beyond the functions with which the instruments are first endowed, so too organisms produce compounds and movements that are responsible for an effect beyond the causal capacities of the compounds as such, the effect being a characteristic operational part of the living entity.

Some instrumental movements are very evident because they oppose the characteristic tendencies of the materials. Particles in fluids tend to diffuse down a concentration gradient, that is, from regions of higher concentration to regions of lower concentration. Organisms, however, can move particles against this tendency by "active transport"; consequently the usefulness of the movement becomes plain and so does the instrumental role of the particles in vital processes.

But there are important differences between artefactual and natural instruments; for entities such as statues, etc., are effects entirely distinct from the principal agents that cause them, as the two do not make one thing per se, whereas the organelles and organs which compounds form are parts of the very thing in which the principal active power is found. Once again, the principal artefactual agent and its instruments are entirely separate from their effect, whereas the active source in the living entity is an inherent power that is not a thing distinct from the organism itself, and this inherent power orders and uses the instruments. Living substances are able to change and modify *themselves* in many ways, and we may define *organism* in general, using this operational characteristic, as *a substance that is able to modify or move itself*.

E. Physical properties as instruments

We have talked about the relation of instrumental physical and chemical activities to the higher operations that are proper to organisms; but in a more general way we may note that most of the qualities common to a class (not those properties that are incidental and peculiar to an individual) are required as instruments for the organism. The passively received modifications which physical properties allow function instrumentally in relation to the principal functions of the organism. Consider, for instance, the following passage:

> Like cartilage, bone consists of cells and an organic intercellular substance (called its *matrix*) which, as in cartilage, consists of collagenic fibrils embedded in an amorphous component. However, the ratio of fibrous to amorphous component in the matrix is much higher in bone than in cartilage, and both the collagen and the amorphous component are somewhat different in composition in the two tissues.[2]

Cartilage and bone, we read, are made of cells put together with an organic intercellular substance, which consists of collagenic (collagen is a kind of protein) fibers that are embedded in an amorphous component. But now we should note:

> Bone is much stronger than cartilage because normal cartilage persisting in the body is not calcified and hence cartilaginous structures of any great dimension would bend if called upon to bear weight. But the matrix of bone is calcified and hence stone-like, so it resists bending and can bear much weight.[3]

As a part of a living thing, bone has a function that requires it to be strong in order to resist the stresses of gravity and other forces; hence the intercellular substance is calcified. Cartilage, however, is a part that has a different function; it must yield in some measure to stress, so its intercellular substance is less calcified. Tendons must transmit the pull of muscles on bones, on account of which they must resist stretching and so have great tensile strength; the lens of the eye must be transparent, which means it is passive to light; the ear drum must be elastic to be moved by vibrations. In all these we see that functions account for physical properties, and ultimately for the disposition of the particle-parts of the tissue, as well as those of extracellular inanimate stuffs that cells produce for their physical properties.

We saw earlier that mental activities present special problems, for we find it difficult to say that impulses are not sensations. But now we are in a position to note that action potentials and other such phenomena in nerve tissue are motion-dispositions in the tissue-subject of the impulse. Though we said earlier that we do not know precisely *how* electrical phenomena are instrumental in relation to sensation, we do know *that* they are. Furthermore, since mental activities are transient in comparison with many other properties of the tissue that are stable, the dispositional electrical phenomena in the tissue-subject are appropriately transient also. The proportion between the transient disposition of the subject and the operation of sensation is evident.

But our observations are not new. Long ago this general state of affairs was recognized by Aristotle, who remarks on it in the following passage:

> Animals, then, are composed of homogeneous parts, and are also composed of heterogeneous parts. The former, however, exist for the sake of the latter. For the active functions and operations of the body are carried on by these; that is, by the heterogeneous parts, such as the eye, the nostril, the whole face, the fingers, the hand, and the whole arm. But inasmuch as there is a great variety in the functions and motions not only of aggregate animals but also of the individual organs, it is necessary that the substances out of which these are composed shall present a diversity of properties. For some purposes softness is advantageous, for others hardness; some parts must be capable of extension, others of flexion. Such properties, then, are distributed separately to the different homogenous parts, one being soft another hard, one fluid another solid, one viscous another brittle; whereas each of the heterogeneous parts presents a combination of multifarious properties.[4]

Heterogeneous parts (organs) are composed of homogeneous parts (tissues) and the organs have multitudinous properties--some of which are opposites--by reason of the various tissues of which they are composed. In all cases the properties are subservient to the functions.

F. Heterogeneous parts and substances

We may not legitimately claim that compounds which are genuinely parts of organisms (not every identifiable compound is actually a part of an organism) exist as separate substances in the organism solely because their physical properties can be distinguished. Individual cells, despite their seeming independence, operate in a coordinated way in tissues and organs; so, too, compounds exhibit their properties within the whole without being separate substances. For although the physical properties of compounds are in the main passive, they are nonetheless coordinated in the functions of the whole through the affections they permit. This is what we expect of an instrument. Just as a piece of sculpture shows the proper cutting effect of the artist's instruments, so in an analogous but not identical fashion the properties of a compound are present in a cell without the molecules being distinct substances. Because of the subordination and coordination of its properties in the whole, *that which we identify as a compound is not complete in species*; the compound has the nature of a part, even though its properties remain when it becomes separated from the whole. To repeat: it is precisely because the compound is a part of a substance and not part of an aggregate that the compound is not complete in species. Here we are faced with a state of affairs that requires the intelligence not to be blinded by appearances. Because the parts are qualitatively distinct, we are inclined to conclude precipitously that they are parts of aggregates. In short, an entity with qualitatively distinct parts endowed with distinct operations is a *heterogeneous substance*.

It is important to emphasize that an organism *must* have qualitatively different parts. Since an organism has several distinct operational capacities (reproduction, growth, self-maintenance), it must also have qualitatively distinct parts. Whenever operations are distinct, the parts in which the operations are found must be distinct in the measure that the operations are; and different operations require different instrumental passivities. We all know that biologists like to say that a living thing must be an organized system, and our aim has been only to point out that the organization belongs to a substance, not to an aggregate. On the other hand, some distinct, identifiable compounds within a cell are not truly parts, and their presence tends to suggest that the organism is an aggregate.

Within cells there are waste materials on the way to being eliminated, as well as food materials not yet assimilated, and neither of these can reasonably be considered parts of the organism. Such substances exist separately in the organism insofar as it is a kind of container and are more like fish in the sea than parts of the cell substance. Furthermore, in multicellular organisms compounds exist that are separated instruments which organisms use, compounds such as gastric fluids that are dumped into the stomach for digestion. So whether a compound or its molecules are or are not parts of the living thing may in many cases be difficult to decide. Nonetheless those that actually are parts owe their properties to the substance of the organism and not to themselves as separately existing entities, as would be the case if organisms were aggregates.

G. A summary

Our point has been to show that the relation between properly biological activities on the one hand and the physical and chemical processes in cells on the other is the relation of a principal operation to its instrumental activities. An instrument is characterized as an agency that is related to an effect that exceeds its own operational capacity, although the instrumental agent does contribute to the effect. As a consequence, the relation between the physical and the mental is not an instance of interactionism in the usual meaning of that word. Nonetheless, each affects the other. The principal agent moves the instrument, and the instrument has an effect on the principal agent insofar as the instrument specifies or determines the action of the principal agent. If this is "interactionism," then the word has acquired an extended meaning.

Notes to Chapter 18

[1]December 1981. Eric I Knudsen, "The Hearing of the Barn Owl."

[2]Arthur W. Ham and David H. Cormack, *Histology*, eighth ed. (Philadelphia and Toronto: J.B. Lippencott Company, 1979), p. 377.

[3]Ibid.

[4]*De Partibus Animlium*, Bk. II, c. 1, 646b 11; from *The Works of Aristotle Translated into English*, J. A. Smith, W. D. Ross, eds. (Oxford: At the Clarendon Press, 1912), Vol. V.

CHAPTER 19

SPECIES, CLASSIFICATIONS, AND DEFINITIONS

A. Gradations in nature

The position we have been arguing implies that substances are graded, some being superior to others, because organisms have the physical properties of inanimate substances in addition to their own operations. Similarly, animals are superior to plants because animals sense as well as reproduce, grow, and maintain themselves.

A Russian biologist attests to this state of affairs in the following passage:

> One organic system is truly superior to another organic system if (a) the first possesses every essential property of the second, but in addition to this relationship of essential similarity or kinship (not to be confused with the relationship of identity) with the latter, it possesses properties which are essentially lacking in the second, whereupon (b) the total of these original properties of the first, with the preeminence of one of them, acts as the leading factor in its internal and external interconnections, that is,

relates to the properties of the second system as major to secondary (and, in the end, better ensures preservation and development).[1]

Although the author employs the term "property" to include properties that are both behavioral and non-behavioral, he supports the position we have presented. He notes that differences in kind depend upon the higher embracing the properties of the lower and adding a difference to them, and the statements he makes are reminiscent of Aristotle.

To show the relations among natural kinds Aristotle compared natural kinds to natural numbers. The natural multitude signified by the number 3 is produced by adding a unit to 2, and 4 is produced by adding a unit to 3, etc. In a similar fashion, a higher natural species adds a difference--a functional capacity--to the characteristics that define the lower; hence the new is not totally different from the old. So because the activities of the higher depend upon the properties of the lower we understand why properties of non-living substances should be present in the living. This subordination of the lower, passive affections to higher operations is the foundation of the gradation of kinds, which implies that *some* "natural species" or "natural classifications" exist; and the behavioral differences we have discussed do provide categories that are naturally distinct. The division of *substance* into *living* and *non-living* is such a classification, as is the division of *organism* into *sentient* and *non-sentient*. Furthermore, there is another animal species that clearly is distinct from others by its fundamental behavioral capacity; of course we are speaking about man, who has the ability to infer theorems from axioms.

But let us not be misunderstood. We are not suggesting that organisms can be arranged in a linear "scala naturae" in which every species is one discrete step up from another, imitating thereby the whole order of the number system. As we have been at some length to say, distinguishing species according to kinds is difficult to do, and a clear delineation of operations would be required for such a linear progression. A clear distinction between the categories of plant and animal can be established on the basis of operations, even though sensation "shades" into purely physical tropisms at its lower limit. But even within the category animal, further distinctions do not readily stand out; at the very least they do not stand out in such a way as to establish a neat, linear order of progression. That the biologist should consider classification to resemble a kind of branching process is understandable. But let us return to a more central issue.

Although classifications on the basis of operations are natural, by themselves they are not adequate for taxonomy. Within main categories, further divisions must be made which are more or less provisional and so "arbitrary." The reason for the variability of such provisional classifications is the difficulty the human mind has in isolating a fundamental, specific behavioral capacity that can divide one class from another on a permanent basis. In principle such capacities would seem to be discoverable, at least for animals, but in practice they remain hidden; and as a consequence, many biological classifications are not considered permanently established.

If, however, one asks what *sort* of behavioral capacity would serve to distinguish animal species further, an answer can be given. In one of his works, E.S. Russell remarks that

we must think of each individual animal as living in its own perceptual world, which is separate and distinct from that of any other individual. No doubt, as Leibniz said, each individual mirrors the same reality, but as the points of view are different, so the perceptual worlds also are different. As there is a diversity of creatures, so also is there a diversity of private perceptual worlds. And the constitution and content of these worlds depend upon the nature of the animal, and vary with its needs and interests. Each animal selects from the possible perceptual environment only those features that are significant in relation to its life and ignores the rest. In this sense each animal makes its own world of perception. . . .

The important thing to realize is that the animal's perceptual world is essentially a practical or functional one. The animal attends to, perceives, and shows behavior in respect of, only those events, objects, and characters of objects that are at the moment functionally important to it, those about

which it is impelled *to do something*; only these have
valence for it. All other features of the environment,
which come within its sensory range, constitute what
we may call the neutral background of action, and in
so far, and at such times, as they are not responded to
or dealt with in any way,they must be regarded as
not perceived, as having no valence.[2]

It is our practice to speak of animals other than ourselves as
"intelligent," but we should be aware that when we do, we extend
the sense of the term. In the passages just above Russell has given
a good description of animal intelligence, telling us that because
each species is different and has its own needs and interests, each
also has a different "perceptual world." Such remarks of course are
not to be construed as a kind of "animal relativism," for Russell
makes it plain that what the animal perceives depends on realities
"out there." From the objective world the animal "selects from the
possible [i.e. total] perceptual environment only those features that
are significant *in relation to its own world of perception* [emphasis
mine]." That is to say, the animal's perception depends upon the
object's proportion (or lack thereof) to the animal insofar as the
object is something the animal either can act on or use in some
way, or insofar as the object can act on the animal. As Russell says,
a species tends to show "behaviour in respect of only those events,
objects, and characters of objects that are at the moment
functionally important to it, those about which it is impelled *to do
something*." In short, the perceptions of the species are practical
and differ according to the different instinctive perceptual
orientations that govern the judgments of the species and control
their experiences in relation to the instinctive behavior patterns
proper to each.

The central point, however, is simply that the cognitive
capacity which in principle might serve to distinguish among
higher animal species is this "practical intelligence" that Russell
describes. Obviously the task is inherently difficult. Could one in
fact adequately characterize the practical perceptive power in the
various species? Only the ethologist might succeed, but I suspect
even so only with difficulty. Still, it seems that that is what we
would have to do to define natural species in a permanent way.
And from this point of view, classifying plants is beyond reach, or

so it seems. We see, then, that even the classification of animals according to clearly recognized, distinct kinds of sensory capacities is very difficult, and remains more an ideal than a working criterion. The many species must be ordered according to criteria that can be actually applied, for instance, anatomical parts, physiological processes, etc., however tentative some of the classifications may be.

B. Definitions: some comments

To the question that asks what something is we sometimes hear the reply "It depends on how you choose to define it," which suggests that the function of a definition is to tell us what a word means. In other words, a definition is supposed to point out the reality to which the word is attached. As we know, words mean different things at different times, and even different things at the same time to different people. On that account, definitions seem to be conventional or stipulative. This appears to be the case especially when the definition determines what it is that is to be investigated. But to regard definitions as stipulative or matters of convention fails to take account of the different kinds of definitions, which is the point we shall discuss here.

If we look at what the sciences actually do, we see that definitions are of two main kinds and are distinguished according to two principal functions. Consider, for instance, what some physicists say:

> The term *fluid* refers to a substance that does not
> have a fixed shape but that is able to flow and take
> the shape of the container.[3]

Here we are told what the word "fluid" means; we are informed about the reality to which it is attached, and that is the function of this definition. But later the same physicists give another definition:

For our purposes we adopt the following definition: A *fluid* is a material substance which in static equilibrium cannot exert either tangential or tensile forces across a surface, but can exert merely pressure (compressive force normal to a surface).[4]

Having stated it, they then add:

From this definition we shall be able to derive all the laws that govern the experimental behavior of ordinary liquids and gases in static equilibrium.[5]

Thus we can see that the second is very different from the first, for its function is to serve as a principle from which the properties of fluids are derived. In other words, the function of this definition is not to attach a word to a reality but to explain the already identified reality's properties.

Chemists do the same sort of thing when they say first that "an acid tastes sour and turns blue litmus red," and then later say that "an acid molecule or ion is one in which the normal electron grouping surrounding some atom is incomplete, and thus the molecule or ion can accept an electron pair from some other atom [the Lewis concept]." The second definition (which actually states not only the definition but also a property that follows on the definition) enables chemists to explain the behavioral properties of an acid, a function the first definition does not perform. In fact, a *perfect* understanding of the second, systematic definition would allow us to explain the more obvious properties in the first definition through which the name is attached.

To illustrate further, we might say that the formula "two-legged featherless tool-making animal" suffices to indicate the meaning of "man." It does not, however, explain man's behavioral peculiarities in the way "reasoning animal" does. If we ask, why is man humorous, able to compose symphonies, weep, speak in artificial languages, etc., we must say it is because he has a rational intelligence; that is, because he is able to grasp and apply general principles to many subject matters and many instances. In other words, the special behavioral properties mentioned depend on the more fundamental, intellectual capacity of the human species that we call "intelligence" or "reason." So here again we have a definition which, if fully elaborated, is capable of an explanatory function.

Our main point can now be made: once the *fundamental* behavioral capacity that accounts for the other characteristics proper to a generic or specific kind has been discovered, the definition is permanent. Suppose, for example that "sentient organism" adequately reveals the basic operational ability of the animal kingdom. And suppose, too, that someone says that deep in a tropical jungle he discovered a plant that said "ouch" when he pinched its leaf and that on that account he claims that the plant has sensation and so the definition of *animal* has to be modified. After all, has he not encountered a plant which is not an animal and which has sensation? But the answer, it seems, is plain enough; for if the leafy thing had a sensory capacity, it would indeed be an animal, its leaves, roots, etc., notwithstanding. Were the objector to continue to insist that the entity was a plant, he would obviously depend upon a definition of plant that employed criteria other than a fundamental behavioral capacity. The definition would be stated in terms of properties much more superficial. In short, once a definition that makes use of the fundamental operational capacity has been assigned to the obvious members of a species, from there on the issue is not whether the definition is to be modified but whether a given case does or does not belong to the class that has been defined. Hence we can make our main point once again: if we could define biological species through their fundamental behavioral capacities, we would have natural classifications expressing permanent kinds or species. But as we saw, not many such are to be had.

Sometimes definitions are rejected because of their difficulty of application in obscure cases. For instance, the dividing line between the living and non-living is hard to locate, as is the line between plant and animal. But such obscurities ought not to cause us to reject the defining criteria, for we would only find ourselves in still greater obscurity.

Sir William Herschel makes our point for us well:

When Dr. H. pursued these researches [on nebulous stars], he was in the situation of a natural

philosopher who follows the various species of
animals and insects from the height of their
perfection down to the lowest ebb of life; when,
arriving at the vegetable kingdom, he can scarcely
point out to us the precise boundary where the
animal ceases and the plant begins; and may even go
so far as to suspect them not to be essentially
different. But recollecting himself, he compares, for
instance, one of the human species to a tree, and all
doubt of the subject vanishes before him.[6]

There is no profit in more words from us.

C. Species variability

The notion that there are permanent species ought not to be
taken to mean that species are invariable. Obvious instances to
the contrary are found in the varying color characteristics of man,
not to mention the various traits in plants and animals for which
breeders are responsible. An invariant definition implies only a
permanence of those characteristics that follow necessarily on the
operational capacity that provides the definition. For instance, a
Euclidean right triangle necessarily has an hypotenuse whose
square is equal to the sum of the squares of the other two sides; and
given the right angle, no other relation of the hypotenuse can be
conceived as compatible with the right triangle. Nevertheless we
could conceive such a triangle as red, green, blue, hot, cold, etc.,
without any similar difficulty. There exist even more profound
contingencies, for when we conceive of an operational capacity that
will allow an animal to move progressively according to its own
desires on the ground, we necessarily conceive of appendages (legs)
that are levers; yet we are not obliged to hold that two is the only
number. Furthermore, the sense of sight does not imply one
specific design of organ, as the actual differences in eyes show; the
same can be said of the sense of hearing. In short, to maintain that
permanent classifications of organisms are in principle, if not in
common practice, attainable, is not to hold to a doctrine of
"immutable essences," whatever that might mean. To be sure, a
great deal more can and needs to be said about this topic, but at

another time and place. These few remarks do suffice, however, to show the main outlines of the position we endorse.

At this point it is perhaps desirable to note that the term "attribute" may be used in a common way to signify that which distinguishes a substance intrinsically as well as a property that resides in the substance. When the occasion requires, however, we shall use the common term when speaking of a difference that distinguishes some category or genus or species. Sentient, for instance, is commonly used to differentiate animals from plants; and when it is so used, it signifies a difference intrinsic to the substance, even though the name first of all derives from sensation, the name of an operation.

D. Species in the realm of the inanimate

Chemists speak about chemical species, and reasonably so. Recalling what we said about elements and compounds, we cannot doubt that the sets of properties which distinguish one stuff from another are causally rooted within the substance and necessarily connected with one another. Consequently, we have to say that where there are different sets of properties there are different substances and hence different chemical species. But when we compare this criterion for determining chemical species with the criterion we used to distinguish biological species, we see that there is a profound difference between them.

Ultimately we tell biological entities apart through their operations; and we distinguish both individuals and species that way. If, for instance, we ask whether a calf born with two heads is one or two individuals, we must reply--assuming both heads to be capable of operations--that there are two calves; for the numerical multiplicity of basic cognitive operations is ultimately what separates one specimen or individual from another in a manner analogous to the way kinds of operation distinguish species. In short, if there are numerically distinct operations of the eyes, ears, internal senses, etc., in the two heads, then there are two individuals. Regarding Siamese twins in the human species, if there are two heads and two sets of ratiocinative activities going on, then there are two individual human beings, no matter how many other bodily parts they may share commonly. But considering kinds of organisms once again, because the unity and distinction of the nature of a class of organisms is established through the unity and distinction of its basic operation, it is plain that biological substances are determinate insofar as they have one operation that accounts for others that are subordinate and for the subservient physical properties as well. In short, the subordination of properties and secondary effect-operations to the one operation that is principal and fundamental shows very clearly the unity and therefore the distinction of the species.

The realm of the inanimate, however, is not the same. We cannot identify a unique ability to undergo the activity of another agent nor for that matter a unique ability to act on another stuff; no one active or passive property determines a genus or species. Thus, we are faced with the fact that inanimate species are indeterminate in comparison to those that are biological. That is to say, inanimate substances do not have a *nature* in the *same* full sense. We must be careful to recognize that the word "nature," as well as the synonymous "species" or "kind," undergoes a shift of meaning when it is applied to inanimate stuffs; and we can see why in the history of modern science it has been so often said that the natural sciences do not know the natures of things. Even in the biological realm where there are natures in the fuller sense and where the ability to reproduce can establish a distinction in kind, we can know the species only to a very limited extent. It is to be expected, then, that in the realm of the inanimate, we cannot go beyond recognizing that substances must be different because their sets of properties are different. One can understand why inanimate substances should be indeterminate in comparison to those that are animate, for the former provide materials for the latter as well as an environment common to the organisms of an ecosystem.

It is, of course, desirable that "nature," "species," etc., be extended to the realm of the inanimate, for we certainly do not want to invent some other words to replace them. So to repeat what we said, elements and compounds are different substances, whether they have natures or species in the fullest sense or not.

Notes to Chapter 19

[1]V. I. Kremyanskiy, "Certain Peculiarities of Organisms as a 'System' from the Point of View of Physics, Cybernetics, and Biology," trans. Anatol Rapoport, in General Systems, reprinted in *Modern Systems Research for the Behavioral Scientist*, ed. Walter Buckley (Chicago: Adaline Publishing Co., 1968).

[2]*The Behavior of Animals* (London: Edward Arnold & Co., 1934), pp. 179-181.

[3]George Shortley and Dudley Williams, *Physics* (New York: Prentice-Hall, Inc., 1950), p. 73.

[4]Ibid., p. 75.

[5]Ibid.

[6]"On Nebulous Stars," *Classics of Modern Science*, ed. William S. Knickerbocker (Boston: Beacon Press, 1962), p. 112.

PART III

THE PRINCIPLES OF SUBSTANCE

CHAPTER 20

OPERATIONAL CAPACITIES AND GENES

A. The Problem

In many ways genes are a center of biological focus, and the issues we are discussing require some understanding of them, for if their functional role is not properly seen, genes tend to be understood in a purely mechanistic way. But before we discuss the central issue, we must say a little about what genes do.

There are many chromosomes and genes in sophisticated organisms, and at one time biologists held that the function of genes was to determine the production of an enzyme: "One gene, one enzyme," they said. More recently they have discovered that many enzymes are polypeptide chains, and each gene controls the production of one polypeptide. An enzyme can therefore be the effect of more than one gene, so biologists now say "One gene, one polypeptide." But whether a gene controls the production of an enzyme, or whether it controls the production of a constitutive protein, does not matter for our discussion here, since both cases exhibit the same kind of relation of the genes to operation. As an instance to be examined, however, we shall use the production of enzymes; for as long as a gene is in some way determinative of the occurrence or non-occurrence of a chemical reaction, its nature, philosophically considered, is the same.

B. Genes as instruments

Enzymes, the biologist says, are biological catalysts, which means that they facilitate chemical reactions in organisms by reducing the amount of energy required to get the reaction going. Catalysts generally do not become a part of the reaction by entering into the product; on the contrary, when the reaction is done, the catalyst's molecules (or atoms) remain unaffected in their constitution. But on the basis of what we saw in the last chapter, this means that enzymes are *instruments* insofar as they bring molecules or atoms together, enabling them to react with one another. On that account, genes, because they control the production of polypeptides that are enzymes or parts of enzymes, are responsible for the production of instruments for chemical reactions, which in turn are instruments for properly biological operations. In other words, genes *presuppose operational capacities* and do not cause them, for we have seen that instruments presuppose the principal agents under which they operate. It has happened, for example, that an induced mutation in *Drosophila melanogaster* has produced a different eye color. The new gene specified a catalyst for a different color; but the new pigment was produced only because the constituents of that pigment were already present. In general, biologists tell us that cells contain the reactants necessary for any or nearly any product any gene might control. Although the point is not germane to our discussion here, it may be said that, given the instrumental character of genes, we ought not to be surprised at their being transferable to other organisms. As long as the reactants required for the compounds they catalyze are present, then the gene can bring about the compound in its new host. Whether the compounds they produce contribute to the welfare of the new host or its species is another matter.

Over and beyond what we infer about genes as instruments on the basis of their determining chemical reactions, the observed behavior of enucleated cells provides empirical evidence for the statement that genes are not principal causes of operational capacities and that the nucleus is not the seat of the latter. By experimenting, biologists have discovered that enucleated cells can carry on certain cellular operations. Speaking of *Acetabularia mediterranea* one author says:

As is well known, anucleate parts still possess marked morphogenetic capacities and are able to form a new stalk, several whorls and even a healthy growing cap. This is especially so if the anucleate part is cut from a plant which is about to produce a cap. The morphogenetic capacity is greatest in anterior parts but nearly lacking in posterior parts.[1]

Acetabularia are able to grow new parts in the absence of the nucleus, from which we see that the operational capacity, although understandably unable to function perfectly, is nonetheless present and so cannot be rooted in the nucleus. That is not to deny the importance of the nucleus; for without doubt it is an essential part cells require for normal operations. Furthermore, the morphogenetic operations described above obviously can occur only as long as the "building materials" are present. Once they are depleted, more have to be produced for further activity, and such production requires the genes of the nucleus. The point, then, is this: from its role in determining basic chemical reactions and the parts and properties which result from them, one may not legitimately infer that the nucleus is the *absolutely first* determinant of the cell's character.

Additional evidence of the relation of the nucleus to operational capacities is provided by cell division in certain organisms. The sea urchin *Arbacia punctulata* has been the subject of a number of experiments, including some that compared the behavior of parthenogenetically stimulated enucleated eggs to other eggs containing a nucleus but treated with actinomycin D:

Enucleated egg fragments stimulated parthenogenetically and thus lacking any nuclear material are called parthenogenetic merogones.

When merogones of *Arbacia* eggs were stimulated parthenogenetically, they formed a fertilization membrane and cleaved. Although the cleavage tended to be irregular and was slower than normal, eventually a blastula was formed that became ciliated, hatched from the fertilization membrane, and made swimming movements for up to one month. This experiment illustrates many important things that we will deal with presently. For the moment, it should be noted that not only was the embryo capable of considerable development, but also it developed better than those possessing a nucleus, but grown in actinomycin D.[2]

The author tells us that the enucleated embryo was capable of considerable development; hence we see that operational capacities were present, including the ability of the fertilized egg to perform the kind of division that is a part of development.[3] Let us look, however, at some additional lines from the same author:

Both types of embryos [those that are enucleated, and those treated with actinomycin D] attain some kind of form that resembles a normal blastula. In other words, cell division can proceed to the point that permits cellular associations that are commensurate with cavitation. Consequently, the division of the cells is not completely disorganized but can still realize some morphogenetic capability. A more important feature of these blastulae is that they are ciliated in both cases. The production of cilia involves the elaboration of specific types of structures that were not present in earlier stages of development. Thus, a new property can appear in a system at the normal time and in its normal morphological dimensions without nuclear contributions. It is also interesting to note that the cilia appear only on the external surface of the blastula, indicating that these cells can recognize their external surface and can establish a morphological polarity in response to it. One must conclude that such a blastula is truly a tissue and not an aggregate, since the intercellular relationships are specifically structured in accordance with a supracellular level of organization.[4]

Because cell division occurs and some development takes place, the empirical evidence would appear to show that operational capacities cannot be rooted in the nucleus, which in turn supports our claim that the role of the nucleus is to provide the necessary instruments required for sustained operations. The nucleus, then, is not the absolutely first determinant of the cell's character but rather presupposes it. And since the nucleus is accessible to observation and experimentation, it is a handle through which we come to understand how functions are carried out.

C. Another word on mechanism

Although we have been arguing against mechanism as an adequate account of natural entities, we would like to say that a mechanism which is only methodological and does not pretend to give a complete account of natural entities, is entirely acceptable. When we consider their investigative field, we see that biologists must explain higher and less common activities through those that are physical and chemical. Certainly biologists do not understand reproduction, that is, mitosis, if they do not understand the necessary instrumental activities the biological operation employs. But inevitably, if that is all they take into account, they must omit part of reality from their considerations. An example will help.

Sight is an operational capacity distinct in kind from vegetative level activities of organisms and distinct in kind from physical and chemical activities. But we can make our point another way by noting that seeing is an activity that requires its own organ as a part in which the operation occurs. Moreover, seeing and its organ are not the same; seeing occurs in the organ but we cannot say it is the organ. Stated this way, the distinction allows us to see the difference between our own considerations and those of the biologist. His investigative field is the organ itself, its parts and their functions; and of course all the functions of the parts are physico-chemical. Biologists do not characteristically concern themselves with the ordinary-experience consideration of sight that we made when we argued earlier that sensation was a distinct kind of activity. And so although such common considerations are necessary, it is also true that a complete understanding of sight requires both an investigation of the operation based on a systematic understanding of common experience and an analysis of the organ and its parts. We see, then, that because biology properly attempts to explain everything it can through chemical and physical activities, it must go about its business *as if the organ were an aggregate*. Stated another way, biology rightly adopts mechanism as a *methodological principle*; for the character of the instrumental activities needs to be known-- down to the elementary particles--if an exhaustive understanding of sight is to be had. A methodological mechanism, however, must not be taken to be a complete theoretical explanation. Mechanism must remain a guiding investigative principle without being erected into a total account.

Notes to Chapter 20

[1]J. Haemmerling, "The Role of the Nucleus in Differentiation Especially in Acetabularia," reprinted in *Molecular and Cellular Aspects of Development*, ed. Eugene Bell (New York: Harper & Row, Publishers, 1967).

[2]Richard Davenport, *An Outline of Animal Development* (Reading, Massachusetts: Addison-Wesley Publishing Company, 1979), p. 99.

[3]Division of a unicellular organism that has been enucleated is not the question.

[4]Ibid., p. 101.

CHAPTER 21

THE INTERNAL STRUCTURE

A. Introduction

In a well known article Michael Polyani describes machines in the following way:

> The structure of machines and the working of their structure are thus shaped by man, even while their material and the forces that operate them obey the laws of inanimate nature. In constructing a machine and supplying it with power, we harness the laws of nature at work in its material and in its driving force and make them serve our purpose.
>
> This harness is not unbreakable; the structure of the machine, and thus its working, can break down. But this will not affect the forces of inanimate nature on which the operation of the machine relied; it merely releases them from the restriction the machine imposed on them before it broke down.
>
> So the machine as a whole works under the control of two distinct principles. The higher one is the principle of the machine's design, and this harnesses the lower one, which consists in the physical-chemical processes on which the machine

relies. . . . But we may borrow a term from physics
and describe both these useful restrictions of nature
as the imposing of boundary conditions on the laws of
physics and chemistry.[1]

The structural harness that man imposes upon materials and
the forces that move them Polyani calls "boundary conditions," and
they are not limited to machines:

> All communications form a machine type of
> boundary, and these boundaries form a whole
> hierarchy of consecutive levels of action.   A
> vocabulary sets boundary conditions on the utterance
> of the spoken voice; a grammar harnesses words to
> form sentences, and the sentences are shaped into a
> text which conveys a communication.   At all these
> stages we are interested in the boundaries imposed
> by a comprehensive restrictive power, rather than in
> the principles harnessed by them.[2]

According to Polyani, any structure or form that determines
something orderable or "harnessable" is a boundary condition.
Furthermore, machines and other artefacts are not the only such
realities, for organisms, too, are characterized by boundary
conditions:

> Any coherent part of the organism is indeed
> puzzling to physiology (and also meaningless to
> pathology) until the way it benefits the organism is
> discovered.   And I may add that any description of
> such a system in terms of its physical-chemical
> topography is meaningless except for the fact that
> the description covertly may recall the system's
> physiological interpretation--much as the
> topography of a machine is meaningless until we
> guess how the device works, and for what purpose.

> In this light the organism is shown to be, like a machine, a system which works according to two different principles: its structure serves as a boundary condition harnessing the physical-chemical processes by which its organs perform their functions. . . .Therefore, if the structure of living things is a set of boundary conditions, this structure is extraneous to the laws of physics and chemistry, which the organism is harnessing. Thus the morphology of living things transcends the laws of physics and chemistry.[3]

Polyani is plain. He claims that organisms surpass non-living entities by reason of their structure, which harnesses the physical-chemical processes by which organs perform their functions. And so the question that must be asked is: what is this structure that surpasses the physical and the chemical, this structure that determines the character of an organism as such? That is the issue now before us, and to it we shall turn, taking it up in the manner our exposition requires.

B. Review of an important point

In chapter 11 we argued that properties are causally rooted in their substances and in chapter 14 that operations are too. The alternative is to say that in non-living substances properties are connected to one another directly without reference to their substance-substratum, and that in living substances operations are similarly connected to one another and to the subservient properties apart from their substance-substratum. But since we are about to argue an issue which takes as its starting point the fact that operations and properties are rooted in substance, we shall perhaps be excused if we reenforce the point with some evidence provided by internal experience.

To begin, let us note that when it proposes hypotheses which postulate theoretical entities, the mind assumes the existence of a necessary relation between operations (or activities or motions) on the one hand and substance on the other. Photons, for instance, are postulated as quanta of energy conceived as existing by themselves and not in a substratum; hence they are conceived as substances. Moreover, motion at 300,000 K/sec is assigned to them as their characteristic property; it cannot be removed without destroying the photons. Thus, a necessary connection between the quantum and its motion is part of the complete conception of a photon, making it impossible to consider one without the other. Were someone actually to claim that he could consider them apart, he would actually be conceiving another kind of entity that is unable to explain the physical effects for which the photon accounts. Stated another way, his new conception would make "photon" an equivocal term, one that at best would belong to some other, perhaps possible, world.

Experiment, too, supports the contention that although photons can be converted to particles, they cannot be slowed or brought to a standstill. On that account these theoretical entities illustrate the spontaneous conviction of the mind that some properties are causally rooted in their substance-substrata. Other elementary entities illustrate the same point. An electron, for instance, is a particle-substance with a charge and spin (however spin is conceived) that cannot be separated from the electron itself.

That operations are rooted in substance is also implied by the experiences we have in controlling our own activities, for whatever else the pronoun "we" brings to mind, it certainly signifies individual entities that do not themselves exist in substrata. And if that which is substantial in *we* is also somehow the source of control, then the operations have to be rooted in the substance. Let it be noted, however, that the proposition is not convertible. We may rightly say "Every quality (the general category of *operation*) under our control is rooted in our substance," but we may not rightly say "Every quality rooted in our substance is under our control."

Evidence showing operations to be under our control is at hand: (1) the occurrence of the operations is not concomitant with the existence of the entity, since operations come and go while the entity remains; (2) the operations are not imposed by extrinsic agents, that is, they are not passively received modifications. Thus our operations are initiated and terminated from within and stem from an active source interior to the substance. To be sure, the presence or absence of the operational *capacity*--not the operation itself-- is not controlled by the substance.

C. The internal structure: its existence

We noted before that organisms are similar to machines insofar as both have heterogeneous parts spatially separated from one another and ordered according to their function. The order in a machine is extrinsically imposed upon materials by a human design which takes advantage of natural properties and uses them for human purposes. Organisms, on the other hand, have an external structure that is not extrinsically imposed and not of human design and not responsible for the operations; so we must now consider what that implies.

An extrinsic structure in an entity of any kind is founded on a multiplicity that is both heterogeneous and ordered; that is to say, a number of qualitatively different parts are put together according to an order to constitute the structure, as for instance, an automobile. Now organisms do exhibit this sort of structure: arms and legs are extrinsic to the trunk, bone is extrinsic to muscle, each is separated from blood vessels, the parts of the digestive system are outside and spatially ordered in respect to one another within the whole, etc. As André Lwoff said, "Biological order . . . is especially a sequence in space and time"; it is an order that cannot be radically changed; for a leg perpendicular to the human back would be useless. Yet the operations themselves, the instrumental physical and chemical activities, and the passive properties subservient to the operations are all rooted in the substance, which brings us to the central point. If (1) an organism's external structure is an ordered diversity of exercised operations residing in a corresponding diversity of ordered parts, and (2) if the operations are rooted in substance, then *within the substance there must be a corresponding order among the multiplicity of operational roots*. Furthermore, since an extrinsic ordered heterogeneous multiplicity of functions and their parts is what a structure is, it follows that *the intrinsic ordered multiplicity of roots is also a structure*, although of a distinctly different kind. At this point the term "structure" has been extended to mean something similar but not identical to the external structure that it originally named. To repeat: the causal roots of operations and the roots of all that goes with them constitute a structure *within the very substance of the organism*. An organism, then, has an internal as well as an external structure, and the internal structure was at issue when

Richard Davenport said (in the preceding chapter) that "the intercellular relationships are specifically structured in accordance with a supracellular level of organization." We now have a new question: what is (the nature of) this "supracellular structure"?

D. Internal structure: its character

To see more fully the character of the internal structure let us begin by examining what biologists tell us about the generation of organisms:

> The ancestry of the millions of somatic cells in a human body can all be traced back to a single cell: the fertilized ovum. Among these millions of cells, about 100 different kinds can be recognized by microscopy. Two processes must therefore occur in the development of the body. First, an enormous amount of cell proliferation must take place, which would require millions of mitoses. Second, as the cells increase in number they must become different from one another. Furthermore, for the body to become composed of parts arranged in a standard pattern with such structures as muscles, tendons, and bones, and such organs as the brain, liver, heart, kidneys, and lungs, all developing in the right places, the cells derived from the fertilized ovum must become different from one another in different sites, in a very orderly way.[4]

Even in very complicated organisms, all posterior cells develop from within a single ancestral cell, and because cellular multiplication and differentiation proceed from a single source, we see that the whole "plan" of a developing embryo antecedently exists in the ancestral cell, a state of affairs for which the biologist has a name:

The word potentiality in ordinary use refers to capabilities not yet realized. With regard to a cell it is used specifically to denote the extent to which it can serve as the ancestral cell for different kinds (not numbers) of cells. Since the fertilized ovum serves as the ancestral cell for all the kinds of cells that develop in the body, it is said to be a totipotential cell. How long does totipotentiality last in its descendants?[5]

Since the ancestral cell serves as the origin of every cell in the organism, it has to possess the operational capacities appropriate to each of the differentiated kinds. On that account, its ability to give rise to every kind of cell is called "totipotentiality," a name that means it can do all things. Totipotentiality, however, does not manifest itself in all cells; for as they become differentiated they ordinarily lose the capacity to become other kinds of cells and are no longer said to have totipotentiality. Yet that cannot be construed to mean that operational capacities originally present have ceased to exist:

. . . it is now generally conceded that, as far as the problem of differentiation is concerned, it is evident that all body cells in the developing embryo and in postnatal life have exactly the same complement of genes. This finding requires some clarification of the meaning of the term potentiality. In common usage, this term does not refer to genetic potentiality but to cell potentiality. The reason for cells losing toti-potentiality as they differentiate is not due to cells losing genes but because the function of certain genes (probably most genes) in the various kinds of cells that develop in a body remain suppressed. For any as yet undifferentiated cell to differentiate into one particular kind of specialized cell, it is essential that the genes it possesses that would direct it into becoming a different kind of cell remain suppressed. For example, if the genes that would direct a cell into developing into, and functioning as, a brain cell, were

also "turned on" in a cell in which the genes that
would cause it to become a liver cell were already
turned on, the results would be chaotic. Hence, for
cells that have complete gene potentiality to become
body cells with restricted potentialities requires that
only certain genes be turned off and for all practical
purposes turned off permanently. This probably
explains why there is so much condensed chromatin
in nuclei; it probably houses the vast number of
genes that are for the most part permanently turned
off in that particular cell.[6]

In differentiated cells, some operations are expressed, while others
are suppressed, which allows us to say that although many
activities do not occur, *every cell has every operational capacity.*
Thus the *entire internal structure with all of its operational roots
has to be present in every cell of the organism,* a proposition that
follows as a conclusion from the biological data. Hence the internal
structure itself is not divisible as a magnitude. (Nor can it be
adequately imagined, though it can be conceived.) When we
remember that muscles, tendons, and bones, as well as organs such
as the brain, liver, heart, kidney, and lungs all develop in the right
places from the cells derived from one fertilized ovum, the
implications are unavoidable. The internal structure with all the
order it represents is originally present in the fertilized ovum and
"passes the whole of itself" to every subsequent part produced from
it. Yet because completed substances are extended, they *must* have
spatially separated physical parts, and for exactly the reason
biologists give: if every operation occurred in every cell, organisms
would be in a state of chaos. In other words, because cells are
virtually (if not actually) totipotential, the orderly exercise of
distinct operations in substances requires spatially separated parts
to prevent the organism from being a mass of confusion. So both
the development and the subsequent exercise of activities of the
organisms make it plain that the internal structure and its
influence extend to every part of the entity.

We can see that the internal structure *is itself unextended*
through another, more abstract argument. Parts that are spatially
separated have their own dimensions and configurations, and we
may convert that proposition: whatever has its own dimensions

and configuration is spatially separated. But because both extension and configuration are properties that reside in substance as a subject, we know that one causal root *within* a substance cannot be spatially separated from others, since what is within a substance cannot be extended. The reason is found in the nature of extension and substance, for that which is interior to a substance is (logically, by nature) *prior* to extension; that is what "within a substance" means. Extension is, as it were, the exterior through which other properties reside in the substance. So, to repeat: an internal structure cannot have parts that are spatially separated from one another because they would have to be extended.

As an illustration closer to ordinary experience that reenforces the notion of an unextended internal structure, we may use the design of a watch in the watchmaker's mind. If he is a good watchmaker, then he will have a complete plan or idea--we are not speaking only of an imaginative picture--by means of which the parts of the watch are conceived in relation to each other and to the whole. But though the design takes account of the parts and their functions, we would not claim that the conception itself of this ordered multitude has spatially separated parts. To be sure, the conception is a kind of mental structure; yet we do not think it to be either a set of ordered bodies or an ordered set of properties determining different bodily parts.

Our considerations now permit us to say that the "boundary conditions" or structure of which Polyani speaks is internal to the substance. Although he himself does not talk about the structure being internal, his description of what the "boundary conditions" do fits the internal structure. His position is but one step away from the one we have defended; for how can a structure surpass the physical-chemical in any other way?

To sum up, then, we may note that we first inferred the existence of the internal structure by starting from the operations and characteristic properties of organisms, and then we described it as consisting of unextended roots or parts which are responsible for the operations and instrumental properties. Having summed up, we may add that because an internal structure is common to living and non-living substances alike, it can be defined commonly as *that by which a substance exists as the kind of substance it is,* and the substance's kind is determined by us from the operations and properties that stem from it. For example, the internal structure of an organism is that by which it is able to reproduce, grow, maintain itself, undergo such and such physical modifications under the influence of such and such external agents, etc. Furthermore, when we say that it is "that by which a substance is," we distinguish it from "that which is," thereby indicating that the internal structure is not the whole substance.

E. Recapitulation

We cannot describe here the many ways one cell or one part of the body influences another and is coordinated with it, for such details are beyond numbering. The professional biologist, who knows them much better than the rest of us, can have a detailed grasp of the internal structures of organisms which we cannot attain, and he is to be envied. Our consideration here has been able to embrace only a little of the data, yet the little is sufficient to show that the source of activities in cells is a structure within the substance of an organism and that it is a unified unextended ordered multitude of operational roots or causes that directs the operations and subordinate activities. The omnipresence of the operational principle implied by totipotentiality is evidence for what we say about the nature of the internal structure.

At this point we ought to recall a few words from Ludwig Von Bertalanffy that were quoted earlier, when he said:

> In order to deal with this [the organization of materials] we are driven, whether we like it or not, to introduce a theory of the structure of living things which surpasses the mere physico-chemical analysis.[7]

A theory of structure--that is indeed fundamental, and what we have attempted to provide.

Notes to Chapter 21

[1]"Life's Irreducible Structure," in *Science*, 21 June 1968, Vol. 160, pp. 1308-12.

[2]Ibid.

[3]Ibid.

[4]Op. cit., p. 166.

[5]Ibid.

[6]Ibid., p. 168.

[7]*Modern Theories of Development*, p. 36.

CHAPTER 22

THE MATERIAL CONSTITUENT

A. The problem

The foregoing chapter argued from properties and operations that are causally rooted in substance to the existence of an internal structure that permeates the whole substance "equally" because the causal roots or parts are not spatially separated. The argument allows a corollary to the effect that one structure is known to differ from another through the operations and/or properties for which each is responsible. On that account, inanimate substances can be known only in a minimal way. Although chemical species are probably distinct, as the way chemists speak about elements and compounds indicates, we cannot claim the same certainty about them that we have about the distinction of the living from the non-living and the sentient from the non-sentient. In short, operations are the primary means by which we know natural substances; properties are secondary to them.

At this point, however, a problem arises; for we must ask some questions about the material "stuff" from which substances come to be. The early Greeks observed that "no entity in nature comes to be from nothing." Put affirmatively this says, "Every entity in nature that comes to be, comes to be from an antecedent entity." We must distinguish, of course, between the antecedent that is a material or materials and the antecedent that is an agent. In the realm of the artefactual, a statue comes to be both from an antecedent block of wood that is a material and from a sculptor who is an agent. But in the realm of the living, one organism comes to be from another that is an antecedent in both respects; that is, the antecedent is an agent, and it also contains the required materials for generation. At the moment, however, we are concerned only with the antecedent that is a material.

In inanimate nature, when salt comes to be, it comes to be from sodium and chlorine, which are plainly materials, even though they are also active in relation to each other. Moreover, when we consider the production of the chemical elements, we see that those of greater atomic weight come to be from elements of lesser weight; helium, for example, is produced from hydrogen. And if we consider the very start of things, the elementary particles themselves come to be from energy, for example, electrons and positrons from photons. The regularity expressed by the Greeks is plainer today than it was in ancient times: when substances come to be, they do not come to be out of nothingness.

This regularity, this general law, gets additional support from an inference that assumes its contradictory: if we suppose that entities in nature do not require antecedent materials, then they will come to be from nothing, which means that salt would not require sodium and chlorine, electrons would not be produced from photons, and oak trees could do without acorns. But we may argue in modus tollens, destroying the consequents on the basis of what we observe.

Yet this does leave us with a problem, one the Greeks put to themselves in the following way: if substance (being) is to come to be, then it must come to be either from substance (being) or from non-substance (non-being), which means it comes to be from nothing. The latter, however, does not happen, so substance must come to be from substance. But what already is cannot come to be; hence substance, which already is, does not come to be. All change, therefore, affects only appearances, only properties, and all things that come to be are property-things. (We have used "substance" instead of "being" because the English term "being" does not here render the correct sense.)

B. The material constituent of substances: first considerations

Once we recognize that substances do come to be and that they require antecedent materials, the problem becomes more determinate. Earlier we argued that salt differs as a substance from both sodium and chlorine, from which it follows that salt cannot come to be from sodium and chlorine taken as substances; for as we said, salt would be an aggregate. Neither can an electron come to be from a photon taken as a substance; nor an organism from proteins, carbohydrates and lipids. A posterior entity that comes to be from an antecedent substance or substances taken as such has to be a property-thing; it cannot be a substance. Antecedent substance-materials would retain their properties and so be clearly identifiable, as they are in aggregates or other property-things. But since none of this is true, then when new substances come to be, they do not come to be from substance-materials, from substances as such. From what, then, do they come to be?

To answer the question, let us begin by noting that although the antecedent substance-materials are not as such the materials from which new substances come to be, the antecedent substances nonetheless provide the materials in some way. Because they come before, and because they are in some way preserved[1] in the new substance (sodium and chlorine can be retrieved from salt, so they are in it somehow), the antecedents must provide the "stuff" from which the new substance comes to be. Hence the question is: precisely what is this material? What is its nature?

C. The material constituent: second considerations

To use an analogy taken from the realm of the artefactual, when a sculptor carves a statue to represent Socrates, say, he begins by obtaining a block of wood or stone of appropriate dimensions; and when the block becomes a statue, the wood remains while the shape of Socrates is acquired and the shape of the block is lost. We call by the name "material" that which endures during the change and which at the beginning is able to become the statue. Before a sculptor begins his work, he knows that a block of wood or stone is potentially a statue by reason of the wood or stone itself and not by reason of the cubical shape. In short, the material is that which is potentially what comes to be. But we ought to observe that a block taken as such is a whole the constituents of which are the shape and the wood, so it is not the *block as block* that can become a statue but the block insofar as it contains a material that can take on the shape of Socrates. So with these points in mind, we are now prepared to consider substances with a view to determining what their coming to be implies about the character of the material they provide. Let us start by indicating the propositions central to the issue.

Substances are similar (but not identical) to blocks and statues in several ways. We have seen: (1) the antecedent substance or substances, like the block, are not as such the materials, yet (2) the antecedent substances are potentially the substance that comes to be. Furthermore, (3) the posterior substance differs from an anterior one through its internal structure: different structures, different substances. Thus the internal structure is a differentiating principle that stands to substance as shape does to block and statue. Also, just as one shape (that of the block) is lost and another is acquired (an image of Socrates), so the internal structures of the antecedent substances must disappear and a new one come to exist in the subsequent entity. From these propositions we come to see that (4) the common material together with the structure compose the substance. Thus because the antecedent substance can become the consequent substance but is not itself the material, it follows that the material is within the antecedent entity and carried over to the posterior. As in artefactual things, so here, too, the material is common. There is no other possible way one substance can come from another.

This point is perhaps most easily seen and most forcefully made by considering the coming to be of one simple substance from another, for example, an electron from a photon. It is probable that these two differ from one another as substances for the reason that photons *must* travel at 300,000 K/sec whereas electrons *cannot*. Such a difference with respect to behavior would seem to justify what we say, especially since it makes no difference to the photoelectric equation. The conversion of energy to mass or mass to energy is indifferent to whether or not electrons and photons differ as substances. Thus we shall assume here that both entities are indeed simple.

If, then, an electron comes to be from a photon or vice versa, there must be something in each that distinguishes them--their own internal structures--and something common to the two that does not distinguish them, namely a material. The necessity of there being such a material is apparent: were there none, the electron would not need the photon and the photon would not need the electron; each would come from nothing. Thus we repeat, the consideration of the production of one simple substance from another imposes on us more forcefully that any other an understanding of the existence of a common substantial material that is not itself a substance.

We might add, too, that this fundamental, substantial material is permanent in the sense that natural processes can neither produce nor destroy it, which is the ground for the instinctive tendency we have to regard substance as permanent. The instinct is not altogether in error, it simply mistakes substance for the material of substances.

But the procedure is not different if we start from examples on a more complicated level, that is, from more complex entities. Ultimately, organisms come to be from organic compounds which their parents ingest; so if we say that organisms come to be from proteins, carbohydrates, and lipids the argument is not different. The amoeba, say, or the chicken, cannot come to be from these aggregated organic compounds as such; each must come to be from them by reason of the material substratum that is within the compounds as an intrinsic part of their substances. If not, then the amoeba and the chicken would be aggregates. But what, now, are the defining characteristics of the substantial material?

First, of course, we must say that it is a part of existing substances, as is the internal structure. The whole substance that comes to be is the thing, and as such it is *that which* (properly speaking) *is or exists or comes to be.* In contrast, a part is not that which (properly speaking) is and so has to be defined in a way that reveals its nature as a part. Thus in the last chapter we defined the internal structure as *that by which a substance is what it is* (the kind of thing it is), a definition which reveals the general nature of the substantial structure through the effect the structure has insofar as it is responsible for something actually existing as a substance of a particular kind. And when the structure is said to be a *that by which*, its nature as a part is signified. The substantial material must be defined in a similar way, so we say it is *that by which a substance can be another*. The definition makes evident the character of the material both as a potentiality and as a part.

There is, however, a precision to be made about this substantial material. When we say that wood or stone can be any one of a large number of artefacts, we say that it can acquire an unlimited number of shapes. But that which a material acquires, it lacks intrinsically; neither wood nor stone has a shape intrinsic to its nature. If it did, then the shape of a sphere, for example, would be present wherever wood was found.

The same thing can be said of the substantial material. If one substance is to become another, then the material must acquire the structure responsible for the new entity, which of course means that in itself the material lacks the structure it acquires. More generally: this material lacks every structure it can take on to become various substances, for that is the very nature of a potentiality, to lack what it can acquire. But a material that is potentially a substance lacking every substantial characteristic (one communicated by the structure) cannot possess any properties either, for every property requires an *actual* substance as a substratum in which to exist. A potential man does not have the shape, size, etc. of a man; nor does a potential horse have the properties of a horse. In short, the material from which substances are produced is a potentiality that lacks the actual characteristics of every substance and so can have no actual properties, no accidents in it. We shall therefore describe it, for want of a better phrase, as an *unqualified potentiality*.[2] Furthermore, insofar as the substantial material is a potentiality for *any* natural substance (following the natural order according to which posterior substances are produced from those that are prior),it is also an *unlimited potentiality*.

It goes without saying that a substantial material cannot be isolated, for that would require it to be an actual substance. Although one substance can be made into another, and that into another endlessly, the substantial material cannot exist by itself and can never be reached by instrumental analysis. Furthermore, like the structure, it permeates the whole. Impossible to imagine adequately and difficult to conceive because of its "next to nothingness" status, the material is, nevertheless, the "stuff"--the word is much extended when used here--out of which any substance, from the simplest to the highest, is made.[3]

We are now in a position to respond to the problem the Greeks posed when they thought substance to be permanent and unable to come to be. Their disjunction was: substance would have to come to be from substance or from nothing. Without taking up all the issues one could discuss in this connection, we may note in answer to their problem that substances come to be, not from some actually existing substance, but from a material within it that, simply speaking, is not a substance, but only a potentiality to be one. Thus, since whatever comes to be must first not exist, all the conditions implied by the coming to be of substance are fulfilled: the substance does not come to be from nothing, for the material substratum lacks every actual substantial attribute; on the other hand, it can become any substance.

D. A recapitulation

The coming to be of one distinct substance from another implies that substances are composed of two principles: (1) an internal structure that is the source of the actual substantial characteristics and the substance's properties; and (2) a material that functions as the subject which receives the structure. It stands to the internal structure in a relation that is analogous but not identical to the relation of a substance to a property. The internal structure is *that by which a substance is what it is*. (This definition can in an extended sense be applied to properties that determine artificial things; for the artefactual structure is *that by which the artefactual property-thing is what it is*.) The fundamental material is *that by which a substance can be another*; it is an unqualified, unlimited potentiality and nothing more.

E. Epilogue to the chapter

Throughout this essay we have developed our position by appealing to observation and natural regularities, saying little about the historical antecedents from which our exposition has profited. So it would seem that now is perhaps the time to indicate that the medieval position on these issues is the one we have put into a contemporary context; and to show that this is so, I shall quote some lines from Thomas Aquinas, which read as follows:

. . .because human knowledge comes to the intelligence from origins in the senses, the early philosophers were preoccupied with sensible realities, slowly progressing to those that are intelligible. And because accidental forms are sensible in themselves whereas substantial forms are not, the first philosophers held all forms to be accidents, and only materials to be substances. Furthermore, since substance suffices as a cause of accidents, which stem from the principles of the substance, the first philosophers proposed no causes beyond the materials [substances]. They held that everything existing in the sensible world came from them. . . . Later philosophers, however, began to consider the forms of substances.[4]

According to Thomas Aquinas, the early philosophers, that is, the pre-Socratics, were mechanists as we have used the term in this essay. Moreover, the term often translated into English as "accident" is what we have called "property," and the term "substantial form" is what we have called "internal structure." But apart from the difference in language, the position we have defended here was that of not only Aquinas but Aristotle before him. Clearly, then, substantial forms are not to be thought of as separately existing immaterial entities, nor is the term "entelechy" rightly understood that way. Language is not the matter of first importance, but it can serve either as a stumbling block or as a source of illumination. On that account, if one wishes to be intelligible to his age, he ought to make use of the contemporary idiom. That is what we have tried to do.

Notes to Chapter 22

[1]We are speaking of a chemical union, not of a separation. Similarly, an organism that dies also undergoes a separation or dissolution.

[2]A substance that can acquire a shape or other properties is not an unqualified potentiality; for in addition to the property-potentiality (or dispositional property) it possesses actual substantial characteristics as well as actual properties.

[3]This material is the "unknowable somewhat" that some thought to be substance. Because the material is an unqualified potentiality, it has no intrinsic knowability. It is knowable only in relation to structure, which it receives. And I wish to remind the reader that the potentiality of a material is not the potentiality of an agent; the former is a potentiality to *be* or become, while the latter is a potentiality to *do*. Between them there is a large gap.

[4]*Questiones Disputatae De Potentia*, q. 3, a. 4.

CHAPTER 23

THE NATURAL AND ITS DISTINCTION
FROM THE ARTEFACTUAL

A. Introduction

In our daily affairs we do not confuse natural entities with those that are artefactual; but philosophical essays sometimes do not distinguish them when they ought, using artefactual entities as illustrations without regard to how they differ from those that are natural. Unhappily such a confusion can have adverse effects, especially when the confusion is not just an accidental slip. Consider, for example, the position a modern author takes:

> The difference between artificial and natural objects seems immediately and unambiguously apparent to all of us.[1]

Having made that remark the author then lists a few entities in each category, after which he declares himself as follows:

> Analyze these judgments, however, and it will be seen that they are neither immediate nor strictly objective.[2]

Jacques Monod tells us that after analysis what at first sight
seems plain is recognized as neither immediate nor strictly
objective, so to him the distinction between artefactual and natural
appears to be unestablished. In succeeding paragraphs he conducts
some "thought experiments" (my use of this phrase) about the
objective properties in terms of which one describes artefacts; and
when, for example, they are compared to a beehive, we find
ourselves confronted with the following:

> We know the hive is "artificial" insofar as it
> represents the product of the activity of bees. But we
> have good reasons for thinking that this activity is
> strictly automatic--immediate, but not consciously
> projective. At the same time, as good naturalists we
> view bees as "natural" beings. Is there not a flagrant
> contradiction in considering "artificial" the product
> of a "natural" being's automatic activity?[3]

In substance, Monod says that we are not able to distinguish
the artefactual from the natural. His ground is that beehives are
artefactual, and to make that assumption he had to have a
criterion already in mind, which obviously is that every activity
that brings about a product is artificial or artefactual. To
understate the case, such a proposition is highly questionable, yet
Monod claims that the difficulty of distinguishing the artefactual
from the natural is grounded in the human intelligence:

> Carrying the investigation a little further, it would
> soon be seen that if there is a contradiction [between
> a product of artificial activity and a product of
> automatic activity], it results not from faulty
> programming [in a computer that makes distinctions
> between artificial and natural objects] but from the
> ambiguity of our judgments.[4]

Our own intelligence is the root of the trouble, for our judgments are confused--ambiguous, if we use his term. And though not many would make Monod's claims, some people do confuse the artefactual with the natural, as is evidenced by the tendency to use artefacts--a telephone, for example--as instances of substance. Discussions of individuation show the same confusion.

The chapters that have gone before showed how artefacts are distinct from substances, and at the end of the discussion they concluded to the principles of such substances, a state of affairs that allows us to say more about the meaning of "natural." Furthermore, not everything that is called "natural" is natural in the same way, for the term has several additional senses under the very general, negative one. We may hardly deny that artefactual things are those which man produces through his intelligence, and such a nominal definition serves adequately as a means for identifying them. Monod, however, implicitly assumes that the definition does not suffice because of the automatic activity found in some organisms other than man. So we must turn to the things we call "natural" to see if we can go beyond the negative description and find what positively characterizes them.

B. Some illustrations of natural properties and natural behavior

For the sake of drawing the reader's attention to the data, that is, to the empirical starting points for the considerations that will follow in later paragraphs, we shall take time to list a few behavioral properties that are rightly called "natural."[5] (A complete catalogue of non-behavioral properties would be difficult to provide, if not impossible; but we can classify them according to the two commonly accepted categories we employed in an earlier chapter, namely, physical properties and chemical properties.) Some commonplace examples are the falling of raindrops or snowflakes, air bubbling up from the bottom of a lake, smoke rising in the atmosphere, cream coming to the top in the bottle of milk. Less commonplace examples are the coming together or moving apart of charged particles, the attraction and repulsion of magnetized pieces of iron, the diffusion of gases through one another, and the dispersion of liquids in a similar way. Chemical reactions are another kind of natural behavior. Except for a few that are largely inert, chemical elements combine to form compounds; they undergo reactions, provided the conditions of temperature and pressure are appropriate. In another realm, organisms maintain and repair tissues, grow, reproduce, move from place to place in a progressive fashion, etc., and these vital activities are familiar to everyone as kinds of natural behavior.

The mind recognizes natural behavior partly as a result of the latter's contrast with behavior that is not natural; for example, a stone rolling up a hill (it is pushed by a small boy), a helium-filled balloon coming down toward the earth (it is on a string and is pulled down by the same small boy), particles of a liquid moving up a concentration gradient, a live rabbit being dragged into the fox's den--the wrong direction from the rabbit's point of view--all of these are examples of non-natural behavior. They are cases in which the entities are said to move under "constraint." Other illustrations could be provided, but these suffice to make our point: some motions are not natural, and they stand in contrast to those that are.

Before we continue, let us note that in another way certain events or occurrences (as well as certain characteristics or properties) are considered non-natural because they are freak events or chance occurrences and not because they result from constraint. Hence, clearing up the ambiguity of "natural" will require us to distinguish the natural from (1) the artefactual, (2) the constrained, and (3) the freak event. The third of these will be considered first.

C. The natural as regular

Taking advantage of those authorities whose business it is to record the conventions of English usage, we may note that the *Oxford English Dictionary* gives an important sense of "natural" when it says the following:

Existing in, or formed by, nature; consisting of objects of this kind; not artificially made, formed, or constructed.

Common usage opposes the artefactual and the natural, and according to such usage realities that are "natural" are "formed by nature." Still, we are not much enlightened, since what it is to be "formed by nature" remains obscure. However, a clue to the further delineation of the notion comes from another meaning of "natural," according to which the term signifies:

> Taking place in conformity with the ordinary course of
> nature; not unusual, marvelous, or miraculous.

This meaning is strengthened by another which is similar:

> Having a usual or normal character (or constitution)
> not exceptional in any way.

Still another listing is plainly related to the two that appear above:

> Having the normal form; not disfigured or disguised
> in any way.

These last three meanings are alike insofar as they all indicate that the natural is something which occurs regularly. Remembering that we first recognize the natural as something not caused by the human intelligence and will, we then add that the natural is usual and not unusual; it does not lack the normal form or character, and it is not disfigured or defective. Thus it is easily distinguished from the freak event, and it serves us as a starting point for arriving at a more systematic definition of *natural*.

If we were to say "The natural occurs regularly in nature," we would use the word in its own definition, which might suggest that we are defining the obscure by the obscure. But that would not be the case, for "natural" has two different meanings in that one sentence, and in the second occurrence "nature" signifies the whole collection of non-artefactual realities with which we are confronted. This is perhaps the most frequent sense of the term, at least in ordinary human life. The first occurrence, however, is the issue. According to it, "natural" signifies *the regular* and so has a more restricted sense according to which it is applied to individual things and their properties within the whole collection of physical realities, which "nature" in the other sense signifies. And so we see that stones regularly roll downhill, that positively charged particles regularly move or tend to move toward others that are negatively charged while regularly moving away from those that are positively charged; we see that distressed elastic bodies such as springs or tree branches regularly assume their original configuration when released, that less dense fluids in a mixture regularly rise to the top, etc. In the realm of the living, plants behave in a regular way according to their species, and so do animals, although the movements of animal species are somewhat variable within limits imposed on them by their instinctive behavioral patterns. In sum, we may say that regularity is the first descriptive characteristic we may assign to the natural, and it serves to distinguish the latter from the freakish, from the chance event.

D. The natural as tending toward a state of rest

In a text on thermodynamics two chemists make some important remarks about natural behavior:

> ... in an early chapter we announced the essential feature of the second law [of thermodynamics] when we stated that every system left to itself changes, rapidly or slowly, in such a way as to approach a definite final state of rest. This state of rest (defined in a statistical way) we also call a state of equilibrium. Now, since it is a universal postulate of all natural science that a system, under given circumstances, will behave in one and only one way, it is a corollary that no system, except through the influence of external agencies, will change in the opposite direction, i.e. away from the state of equilibrium.

Many types of processes leading toward equilibrium are familiarly known. The diffusion of material from a concentrated solution into a diluted solution, leading toward a condition of uniform concentration; the passage of heat from a hot body to a cold body, leading to uniformity of temperature; the oxidation of organic substances by the atmosphere ... are all processes which illustrate the kind of change that occurs spontaneously in nature. ... These processes and all other natural processes are alike in one respect, that they are bringing the various systems toward the condition of ultimate equilibrium or rest, and we may think of these systems as thereby losing in some measure their capacity for spontaneous change.[6]

As the reader can see, Lewis and Randall regard natural behavior as tending toward a determinate end state, and we may add that what they say about physical and chemical activities is true of the behavior of living things as well. The stone that rolls downhill comes to a stop, charged bodies come together and then approach each other no longer, the elastic body (perhaps after oscillating) finally comes to rest in its original configuration, cream stops at the top of the bottle, a gas no longer diffuses into another when the mixture is uniform, chemical reactions form no additional amounts of the compound when equilibrium is reached, etc. In the category of the living, reproduction stops when mitosis is completed or when the new multicellular organism is formed, tissue repair stops when the wound has healed, digestion stops when there is no more food in the stomach, the nest-building activity stops once the nest is completed, and so it goes. Although many animals go continually from one activity to another, each of their actions has a definite term. Moreover, some activities are ordered integrals containing many lesser actions as parts, for example, the cutting and hauling of a tree by a beaver, while others are integral insofar as they require the cooperation of a number of individuals, for example, the construction of a dam by a colony of beavers. Yet whether we consider the parts or the whole, induction allows us to conclude that all natural actions come to a terminal state, which on the macroscopic level is called "rest" and on the level of atoms and molecules is called "equilibrium." The difference in the signification of these two terms in this context comes from the difference between the part and the whole: we call the final state "rest" when we look at the whole; we call it "equilibrium" when we look at the parts apart from the whole they constitute. Hence the two terms are not opposed but complementary, for a whole can be at rest even though in another respect its parts may be moving within it. In short, when Lewis and Randall draw attention to movements as tending to a state of rest, they point to an important aspect of natural behavior.

In order to emphasize that a state of rest is realized differently in different kinds of natural behavior, we should note that even the physiological components of gross behavior reach a state that is legitimately called "rest." If a red-blooded animal hemorrhages, its body begins to produce red blood cells until a normal count is reached, and then the cell-producing activity ceases. People who engage in strenuous exercise begin to perspire when their body temperature rises, yet the perspiring stops when the temperature is reduced. So both gross behavior itself and the behavior of its physiological components are characterized by an end state that is rest. (Of course, there are certain energy-supplying and other chemical activities that go on constantly because the deterioration in living things requires them.) Thus we are now able to assign two attributes to natural behavior: it is regular, and it also tends to a state of rest. But we are not yet able to distinguish the natural from the artefactual, for the latter, too, can be said to be regular. On that account the section that follows bears more directly on the central issue.

E. Spontaneity

As the reader will recall, Lewis and Randall speak of natural behavior as spontaneous, and the quotation that follows underlines the point:

> If a system is at equilibrium, no process tends to occur spontaneously and there is nothing to harness to produce work. A ... mechanical example is the production of hydroelectric power. Here work is

obtained when the spontaneous tendency of water to flow from a high to a low level is used. Lord Kelvin's statement recognizes that the spontaneous process is the flow of heat from a high to a lower temperature and that only from such a spontaneous process can work be obtained.[7]

The notion of spontaneity is important for chemistry, and it took some time for chemists to define a spontaneous chemical reaction to their satisfaction. But the notion is not restricted to chemistry, as the following text by a physicist shows:

... "weak interactions" [are] responsible for radio-activity, the spontaneous change of one atomic nucleus into another with the emission of an electron or positron.[8]

Less esoteric examples also show our use of "spontaneous" in connection with the natural; for we speak of water spontaneously flowing downhill, of non-miscible fluids spontaneously separating into layers, of charges spontaneously attracting and repelling each other, of water spontaneously freezing at cold temperatures. (Not only are *motions* said to be spontaneous, so are the *tendencies* things have to move when conditions are right.) And since we also speak about the spontaneous behavior of animals, including certain actions of our own, there is little doubt that we use the term in connection with natural behavior. So the question now becomes: what is the meaning of "spontaneous" according to the conventions of usage?

The *Oxford English Dictionary* tells us that the first sense of the term is:

Arising or proceeding entirely from natural impulse, without any external stimulus or constraint; voluntary and of one's own accord.

As we all know, our peculiarly human activities are under our own control, so we are self-determining in a way that is not fully shared by any other species. According to the limitations imposed by circumstances, men may select their own occupational behavior, as well as the environment and other means by which they intend to pursue it. This mode of living we call "voluntary," and it issues from our own judgments and intentions. In this respect actions that are voluntary are opposed to those we do under constraint, and a number of terms function as synonyms for "to constrain," among them "to force," "to compel," and "to coerce," all of which are opposed "to act spontaneously."

The second meaning of the word "spontaneous" is akin to but not identical with the first, and it signifies:

> Arising purely from, entirely determined by, the internal operative or directive forces of the organism.

Here the word retains the notion of interior origin but omits the notion of voluntary control, which is to be expected when the word is applied to organisms generally.

Not unexpectedly, "spontaneous" has a third signification according to which it is extended to inanimate entities:

> Occurring without apparent external cause; having a self-contained cause or origin.

This meaning omits the notion of internal operative or directive force; yet the spontaneous is still described as issuing from a self-contained, internal cause or origin. Hence in this sense the spontaneous is that which occurs without an apparent cause, and it draws attention to an important point. Although gravitational and electromagnetic movements, for example, result from external gravitational and electromagnetic forces, the latter are not apparent, they are not observable. We have, then, a broader sense that is important for all natural sciences; for as Lewis and Randall said, "at equilibrium, no process tends to occur spontaneously." At universal equilibrium, there would be no natural changes. But now to what is essential.

Whether animate or inanimate, no spontaneous movement as such results from an observable cause because "spontaneous" in every one of the senses listed signifies that which issues from *within* the entity that is moved, modified, or changed in any way; it signifies that which has an internal origin that is unobservable, whether or not some cooperating external force or cause is observable. The very notion of *within* implies external unobservability, for the *within* is inaccessible to external observation except when we can penetrate or get around what is without, which we can do when the exteriority-interiority difference is spatial. In contrast, the *within* of a substance is not spatial and is not attainable through observation. Yet aided by inferences, we do understand what "within" means when it is a question of animals, plants, minerals, and other natural entities. Of course the inanimate has "less" of an interior than the animate, plants have "less" of an interior than animals, and non-human animals have "less" of an interior than man. That, however, is not relevant to determining the meaning of "spontaneous."

F. The ways of being spontaneous

Organisms are the kind of natural entity that most obviously has an internal principle of behavior, for an organism moves itself insofar as its operations are started and ended from within. Plants reproduce, but they are not always reproducing; they repair tissue but are not always repairing; they grow but are not always growing; animals move about but are not always moving about, etc. After such operations have begun and the appropriate end states reached, the operations are turned off from within the organism itself. In short, organisms exercise a (sometimes very limited) control over their own activities. Jacques Monod himself makes this point when he speaks of an organism as "self-constructing":

> ... a living being's structure results from a totally different process, in that it owes almost nothing to the action of outside forces, but everything, from its

overall shape down to its tiniest detail, to
"morphogenetic" interactions within the object itself.
It is thus a structure giving proof of an autonomous
determinism: precise, rigorous, implying a virtually
total "freedom" with respect to outside agents or
conditions--which are capable, to be sure, of impeding
this development, but not of governing or guiding it,
not prescribing its organizational scheme to the
living object. Through the autonomous and
spontaneous character of the morphogenetic
processes that build the macroscopic structure of
living beings, the latter are absolutely distinct from
artifacts, as they are, furthermore, from the majority
of natural objects whose macroscopic morphology
largely results from the influence of external
agents.[9]

He who said that we cannot tell the artificial from the natural
could not have distinguished the natural better.[10] In particular,
his insistence on "freedom" from the influence of extrinsic agents is
by itself sufficient to show that organisms cannot be artefacts; for
the latter have no spontaneous operations or movements of their
own, but only those that belong to the materials out of which they
are made. But the main point is that the spontaneous behavior of
organisms originates from within them insofar as the organisms
initiate and terminate their own activities; that is, insofar as
organisms turn their own operations on and off. Their spontaneous
activities are those of agents.

Although chemical elements are not living substances, and
although chemical reactions require appropriate conditions of
temperature and pressure, many elements react spontaneously
under the appropriate conditions to form compounds; that is, they
mutually react on one another by reason of principles internal to
their substances, and this is a second kind of spontaneity. The
mutual ability of elements to *undergo* the activity of others is
indeed a spontaneous tendency to produce new substances. (More
technically, a reaction is spontaneous under given conditions of
pressure and temperature, and only if it makes free energy
available for useful work. But this does not deny what we say;
rather it presupposes it.) But let us now look at purely physical

movements for a kind of spontaneous behavior which differs from that of chemical change, considering the latter insofar as it brings about different substances and ignoring the physical modifications that accompany those changes of substance.

If one places pieces of various kinds of metal near a magnet--for instance, copper, silver, lead, aluminum, gold, iron--he finds that only iron spontaneously moves toward the magnet. The others remain at rest. From this we infer that iron is dispositionally (passively) oriented toward being affected by the magnet and that iron tends to become magnetized in the presence of a magnetic field; and certainly the disposition, the passivity, is real. Thus iron is rightly said to move spontaneously, although the spontaneity is less perfect than the spontaneity that characterizes organisms, since iron is only passively affected by the magnetic field. Charged bodies are similar in that they can be affected by other bodies that carry charges. In short, an internal disposition to be moved by another is required as a cooperating principle for certain motions; and, if the disposition is regular, it has to be rooted in the substance, otherwise it could be made to come and go in the way of shapes and artefactual structures.

Even gravitational motion, the most universal in nature, requires an internal, cooperative disposition or passive principle to account for a body's tendency to be moved by a gravitational field; for unless a thing has mass, it cannot undergo gravitational attraction. For many years light was thought not to have mass and so to be unaffected by gravity, but physicists now know that it bends in a gravitational field and consequently must have mass. A neutrino, on the other hand, is said not to have mass and so to be immune to the effects of gravity. Our point, then, is this: the physical modifications that inanimate entities naturally undergo require internal passive, dispositional roots or principles within the substance to account for their regular modifications. Hence we may repeat: although passive behavior originates less perfectly from within because it depends on an external source of activity, it nonetheless is rightly said to be spontaneous.

Other movements are spontaneous in a third way. If, for instance, one asks a physicist what would happen to a photon were it to slow down, his reply will be that it cannot be slowed down. As long as the photon exists it moves at 300,000 kilometers per second and cannot be inhibited, which means that the motion of the photon is conceived as stemming necessarily from an internal principle; the two--the photon and the motion--must occur together. A photon is not moved by some kind of attraction or repulsion or by some kind of pushing or pulling; the coming to exist of the photon suffices for it to have its motion, and as long as the photon exists, so does the motion. Consequently, destroying the motion requires destroying the photon.

An example on the macroscopic level that is similar in part to those we have just discussed is the diffusion of a gas. As soon as a gas exists it tends to diffuse through another. And though inhibiting the diffusion does not destroy the gas, its motion is nonetheless like that of a photon insofar as the motion exists as soon as the gas exists, provided there are no impediments. But as the last clause indicates, to the extent the diffusion can be impeded it is unlike the motion of a photon.

We may now summarize and say that behavior can originate from an internal principle in one of three ways: (1) actively, as is the case with organisms, which initiate and terminate their own operations; (2) passively, as is the case with inanimate entities that have a disposition to be moved, and to cooperate with an appropriate agency that does the moving; (3) formally, as is the case with bodies which as soon as they exist either move or tend to move independently of being pushed or pulled, attracted or repelled, by an external agency. There are three ways, then, in which a motion can be spontaneous and therefore natural.

At this point we may note that no machine or ordered aggregate can be the subject of behavior that is truly spontaneous. "Self-regulating" or "self-moving" machinery has a source that is "internal" only insofar as "internal" means "spatially within" certain confines. In short, no self-moving aggregate has activities that originate from within *in the way the activities of an organism do.* The only truly spontaneous activities a machine could possibly have are those that belong to the natural substances that are its materials. The behavior of a machine is extrinsically imposed on its working parts.

G. Constrained motion

We should recall the words of Lewis and Randall when they said:

Now since it is a universal postulate of all natural
science that a system, under given circumstances,
will behave in one and only one way, it is a corollary
that no system, except through the influence of
external agencies, will change in the opposite
direction, i.e. away from the state of equilibrium.

To the extent that a system is natural it behaves under given
circumstances in one and only one way, and that, the authors say,
is a universal postulate of natural science. Only under the
influence of external agencies can a system change in the opposite
direction, and such motion we shall call "constrained." To throw
light on its characteristics, we need to consider again (1) what a
system is; (2) what is meant by an opposite direction; and (3) the
character of the constraining agency as well as the passivity for
constrained motion.

(1) As we saw in an earlier chapter, if one considers a solitary
body, disregarding all others, he does not have a system; but if he
takes into account at least one other body with which the first
interacts, then he has a system. A system, then, requires both a
body that is a passive recipient and another that is an active
agency, each proportioned to the other. (Of course a system can
consist of more than two bodies.) That is our first point.

(2) When we reflect on the spontaneous motion of a falling
stone, we readily see what is meant by an "opposite direction," for
the plainest case of the latter is a motion of a stone along the path
of the falling body but going up from the surface of the earth
instead of down. To move that way the body must be affected by
some agency opposed to gravity that is outside the system
constituted by the body and the earth, and so the motion is
constrained. But physicists tell us that if we draw a line from the
center of mass of the falling body to the center of mass of the earth,
then any falling motion that deviates from this line does so only
because it is affected by something that is outside the system. (If
the system had three bodies, say, then a constrained motion would
be a non-gravitational deviation from the path demanded by the
interaction of the three.) Consequently an "opposite direction"
must be taken to mean any deviation from the direction of the

spontaneous motion, and we can not know what is *opposite* or *constrained* until we know what is spontaneous.

Another illustration of constrained motion, one that does not involve a gravitational system, is the motion opposed to the diffusion of a gas. As we know, the end state following on diffusion is a mixture; so any motion that consisted in the separation of one gas from another and was followed by a reduction in the volume of the separated gas would be constrained. Clearly such motion would have to come about as the result of the action of a cause extrinsic to the system of gases. Speaking more generally, any motion of a fluid that is up, not down, a concentration gradient would be constrained.

Living things can undergo constrained motions too. An oak tree that grew horizontally would be constrained by something, for oak trees regularly grow upward; a rabbit moving into a fox's den would probably be dragged there against its "will" by the fox, since ordinarily the rabbit's interest is not promoted by its entering such a place. Thus, motions opposed to the instinctive behavior patterns of animals and the innate tendencies of plants ordinarily result from what are by definition constraining agents. (We need not consider the abnormal behavior that results from pathological states in living things.) In sum, *opposite* must be defined in relation to *spontaneous*.

(3) We may now state expressly the characteristics of a constraining agent, namely that the extrinsic agent of which Lewis and Randall speak is an agent outside the system or entity being considered, and it opposes the innate tendencies of the members of the system. Every passive spontaneity corresponds to some natural agency, and together the two produce what we call natural motion, as our illustrations earlier have shown. So we already know that in regard to passive spontaneity a constraining agent is any agent not directly proportioned to the innate orientation of the recipient, and extrinsic to the system. Similarly, if the motion is formally spontaneous and occurs or tends to occur (unless impeded) as soon as the thing or stuff exists, then again a constraining agent is one that opposes the formally spontaneous motion and is outside the spontaneously moving entity; here we do not need a system. To illustrate, we again point to the diffusion of a gas or to the dispersion of a liquid. Furthermore, let us not forget that plants and animals are also subject to constraint by extrinsic agents. A question remains, however, as to what sort of passivity bodies have

in the face of constraining agents. How does a natural, spontaneous, passive disposition differ from the ability to be moved against an innate tendency?

As we all know, a stone can be thrown in many directions by men, volcanoes, strong winds, etc.; so it possesses a passivity *of some sort* for constrained motion. Yet there is no doubt that the passivity is unlike that of the stone to be moved by a source of gravity. To put the matter more succinctly: since we recognize a constrained motion because it is *opposed* to one already known to be natural, we see that the constrained body cannot have an intrinsic, constitutional disposition toward the constrained motion; for no entity can simultaneously have an internal disposition to move one way and another internal disposition to move in an opposite way. On that account the passivity of bodies in respect to constraining agents cannot be rooted in the principles of the species as such but is the result of the inability of the passive principle and the corresponding agent to determine completely the motion; that is, the inability of the natural determinants to move the body in an absolutely necessary way makes constrained motions possible. A passivity for constrained motion is not a cooperating principle; it merely renders the body "submissive" to the action the agent. An analogy can be seen in the case of constrained human actions. If we are literally dragged someplace against our efforts and desires, the motion in no way stems from an internal principle. It is solely the consequence of our inability to guarantee completely the carrying out of our self-originating actions.

H. "Mixed" cases

It might seem that some motions are both spontaneous and constrained. For instance, a rabbit that hops about is said to behave spontaneously insofar as the rabbit itself is responsible for the hopping; yet if the rabbit hops up a hillside, is not the upward motion against gravity and therefore constrained? The answer requires, of course, a distinction; for if we consider the rabbit generically according to its mass, according to that which it has in common with all other bodies, then the upward motion is indeed constrained. But if the rabbit is considered according to its specific character as a four-legged mammal of a certain classification, then the hopping is spontaneous and natural.

The same distinction can be made in the realm of inanimate things. Since gravitational attraction exists between any two bodies or particles whatsoever, gravitational movement must be regarded as the most generic of spontaneous motions. On the other hand, because electric charge is not common to all bodies or particles, the spontaneous movements to which a charge gives rise are more specific; they belong to a subclass of bodies. Thus a movement of charged particles against gravity is spontaneous if we consider the charged particles according to that which is proper to them as charged entities. And so in the proper sense, a motion or kind of behavior is judged natural when it is considered in relation to the proper class of entity to which the motion belongs. That which is natural to a genus will not be natural to a species, and conversely. And so we now see the character of constraining agents, as well as the passivity for constrained motion.

That machines are characterized by constrained motions is now apparent. They must make use of some spontaneous active capacity or capacities provided by nature, and "harness" them by imposing artefactually directed motions on passive parts. That is essentially what human art and engineering skills accomplish: the production of artificially directed, constrained motions for human benefits.

I. Other senses of "natural"

There is another distinction to be made regarding the natural. The notion of natural as inborn or spontaneous is most properly applied when we consider that which follows on the nature of the class and is found in every member of it. However, some properties are limited to populations that are less than the entire membership of the class, for instance, skin color in the human species. We do tend to speak of skin color as natural insofar as it is in us from birth and is not an acquired trait; but since the same color is not common to the entire species, color cannot stem from the principles that constitute the species as such. Similarly, some people are naturally more athletic than others, some have musical talent, etc., and these traits, too, are natural in a lesser sense, insofar as they are inborn but do not issue from that which defines the species.

There are, then, diminished senses of "natural" that ought not to be confused with the natural that is intrinsic as a constituting principle of the class and responsible for that which is regular for the entire species.

J. The per se and the incidental

The last point we have to make in connection with the natural is that it must not be confused with something that is incidental. Suppose that Socrates is both a physician and a carpenter and that he built his own house. Under those circumstances we could formulate the proposition "The physician built a house." But we all know that the physician does not build a house by reason of the art of medicine but by reason of the art of carpentry he happens to possess. In this case we can say that the physician is an incidental cause of the house; and when we say he is incidental we indicate that the art of medicine is in the same subject as is the per se cause, namely, the art of carpentry. So if, for instance, we were to say that two-eyed mammals naturally swim we would have confused something incidental with the natural as it is strictly defined. And were we to consider Socrates as a physician who cures himself, his curing himself would not be natural just because the cause of the motion and the recipient are in one and the same entity. The art of medicine is acquired by Socrates and is only incidentally in him as a cause of his being healed. That is not to deny that medicine is a per se cause of healing; it is only to point out that medicine is incidentally in Socrates and that the physician cures himself only incidentally, whereas an organism that increases its own size through growing does so per se. The truly intrinsic natural principle of Socrates' being healed is his active capacity to fight infections and other afflictions, which the art of medicine aids as an instrument.

The search for the per se, the relevant, is of course what is formal to natural investigations. If we were to think that cigarettes cause lung cancer because the tobacco is brown or shredded, we would have fastened on the incidental instead of the per se. When Gilbert concluded that bodies capable of being electrified were solidified liquids, he confused the per se with the incidental. But we may expect that this sort of confusion about the natural is not likely to arise often.

K. A definition of the natural

From the considerations we have made above, we are now able to formulate a definition; but before we do, let us list the relevant defining elements according to the order in which we discussed them.

(1) A natural movement is one that is regular; it belongs to all or to most members of the species (some individuals may be defective).

(2) Natural behavior or motion tends to a determinate state of rest, which is a determinate end state or entity.

(3) A natural motion is spontaneous, which means that it issues from within the substance. There are three ways in which behavior can be spontaneous: (a) by reason of an internal active principle; (b) by reason of an internal passive principle; (c) by reason of a formal principle, when the motion issues from the substance in the manner of a necessary property. Every behavior that comes from an internal principle is rooted in the structure of the substance, except the capacity to become another substance, which is rooted in the fundamental material. To repeat: the passive capacity to become another substance is the only capacity rooted in the material; all others, which are properties, are rooted in the internal structure, including the passivities for physical modifications. So if we know or hypothesize about what is natural in the strict sense, we know or hypothesize about the behavior that characterizes a class, either generic or specific.

(4) Natural behavior is *first* in the sense that it is proper to the class in which it is found; that is, a kind of behavior is said to be natural when it is convertible with the class in which it occurs. For instance, diffusion is natural to gases, for every gas diffuses, and everything that diffuses is a gas (liquids do not diffuse in a strict sense, since they are bounded by a surface). Or we might say that sensing is natural to animals because every animal senses and every organism that senses is an animal. Hence to signify this commensurability of the behavior with the class, we shall say that the motion or behavior which *first* belongs to the class is natural in the most proper sense, while other properties are natural in a diminished sense that must be distinguished from the one that is primary.

(5) Natural movements in the proper sense are per se (relevant) to the class; that is to say, nothing that is incidental is truly natural in any proper sense of the term.

With the defining elements now listed we may state the definition of natural motion or behavior (and secondarily of natural property) as *a regular motion or behavior that tends to a state of rest and issues from a principle or cause that is within, first, and per se.* And since "nature" is the noun signifying the internal principle itself, we ought to remark that "nature" as so signifying is not equivalent to "nature" as meaning that which is made known by a definition telling us the what-it-is of a class of substance. The latter is yet another meaning of the term.

L. Recapitulation

In many respects it might seem to have been unnecessary to discuss at length the notion of the natural in order not to confuse it with the artefactual. Yet given Monod's remarks, together with the tendency of mechanism to view natural things as the same kind of aggregate as those that are artefactual, we think it has been a useful pursuit. Artefacts are not natural because the properties that specify them as artefacts originate from without, and the movements that belong to artefacts are constrained; that is, they are directed in ways that exceed the natural. What is natural originates from within the substance, from its internal structure; or if the natural behavior is the becoming of another substance, then it is rooted in the substantial material. Furthermore, the natural in its strictest sense is convertible with a given class. It is also true that some properties that are inborn do not have their root in the class as such but in individual differences which are more or less extensive in the class-populations.

Notes to Chapter 23

[1]Jacques Monod, *Chance and Necessity*, trans. Austryn Wainhouse (New York: Vintage Books, 1972), p. 3.

[2]Ibid.

[3]Ibid., p. 6.

[4]Ibid., p. 7.

[5]In philosophy it is conventional to use the terms "motion" and "movement" to signify any kind of change in nature, and we shall employ the words in that sense here.

[6]Gilbert Newton Lewis and Merle Randall, *Thermodynamics*, 2nd ed. (New York: McGraw-Hill, 1961), p. 76.

[7]Gordon M. Barrow, *Physical Chemistry* (New York: McGraw-Hill Book Company, Inc.), 1961, p. 131.

[8]Robert H. Dicke, *Gravitation and the Universe* (Philadelphia: American Philosophical Society, 1970), p. 1.

[9]Op.cit., pp. 10-11.

[10]The paragraph quoted above continues with the following lines: "To this there is a single exception: that, once again, of crystals, whose characteristic geometry reflects macroscopic interactions occurring within the object itself. Hence, utilizing this criterion alone, crystals would have to be classified together with living beings, while artifacts and natural objects, alike fashioned by outside agents, would comprise another class." But he does not make his point, he has equivocated on "within," as anyone familiar with our earlier consideration of organisms as substances will know.

THE NATURAL AND THE ARTEFACTUAL COMPARED: AN EPILOGUE

The considerations we have made during the course of this essay have allowed us to see that there is a fundamental difference between the natural and the artefactual, not to mention natural entities that are aggregates. Whatever is artefactual, however, has its origin from outside, supposing in the materials only a capacity to receive the activities directed by human intelligence. This difference between the internal and the external is profound. Were the design of a machine, say, to become internalized within the substance, then the machine would be a natural entity and, if self-moving, alive. Put another way, the spatial organization and structure of a machine directly reflects an internal "plan" that in many ways does resemble human design. This mutual resemblance is especially evident when an organism, frustrated by some obstacle in its attempt either to form or to reconstitute some part, employs another, unusual procedure for attaining its goal.

Looking again at the activities of the two kinds of entities, we see that the difference between them is manifest in the relation of one activity to another. The activities of an organism, say, are hierarchically ordered, the lower functioning as instruments of the higher. When this is the case there are constrained motions that are the consequence of the inferior movements being directed in ways that exceed the inherent operational powers.

Artefacts, on the other hand, though they have directed activities which are constrained motions, are nonetheless systems of a different kind; for in them one part acts on another in a serially related causal chain, which depends solely on the application of active properties to others that are passive. There is nothing in the least internal about the structure of a machine or other artefact.

That, then, is the fundamental error of mechanism or reductionism: all natural entities other than elementary particles, because they are not substances, have only external principles. Plainly the notion of substance is important for philosophy and for our understanding of the world of nature. Without a sound conception of substance no satisfactory account of natural entities and natural phenomena can be given. As an issue about the real world, substance is first of all a natural, not a metaphysical consideration.

APPENDIX

ARISTOTLE'S ARGUMENT

A. Introduction

Chapters 22 and 23 have been concerned with the intrinsic constituting principles of natural substances, and their discussions aimed at distinguishing the internal structure from the substantial material with a view to showing the role of each both in the composition of the substance and in the latter's coming to be; so the first twenty-one chapters constitute a preparation without which the substantial structure and material would not, in my judgment, be intelligible. But the argument for the distinction of these principles was first put forward by Aristotle more than two thousand years ago,[1] and in order to give him his due, I wish now to repeat what he did by presenting his argument in his way. I must add, too, that my presentation will include comments that are dependent upon the commentary Thomas Aquinas made upon Aristotle's exposition.

B. Aristotle's argument: the number of principles

As we know, all motion has two terms, a term *from which* (a quo) the motion proceeds, and another, a term *to which* (ad quem) it proceeds or tends. Both of these terms can be signified either simply or complexly, which allows us to talk about coming to be in two ways. We may say, for example, that *the man becomes skilled*, and in so speaking we signify each term simply. The same is true when we say that *the non-skilled becomes skilled*, for here again each term is signified simply. Both the term *from which* and the term *to which* signify simply in these propositions because only one notion is explicitly manifested or brought to mind by each of the words "man" and "non-skilled." Aristotle named the two terms differently, calling the term *from which* as signified by "man" the *subject*. The term *from which* as signified by "non-skilled" he named the *opposite*, while the term *to which* as signified by "skilled" he named the *term*.

The coming to be may also be signified in a complex way; for we may say that *the non-skilled man becomes a skilled man*, and when we do each term is signified complexly. Both the term *from which* and the term *to which* are signified as composites of two simple notions or formalities. Moreover, the simple and complex terms may be combined in several ways. We may say that *the non-skilled man becomes skilled*, or *the man becomes a skilled man*. But the points to be emphasized are (1) that each term may be signified either as simple or as complex; and (2) the term *from which*, the antecedent, may be signified simply either as "man" or as "non-skilled," one of which is affirmative and the other negative. That we may speak this way is a matter of our experience with our language. (We have already seen that a single term can signify a complex reality, as for instance, "carpenter" or "grammarian.")

Although becoming is attributed to the antecedent under the names "man" and "non-skilled," experience reveals that there is an important difference in what is signified by each; for that which is signified by one, "man," is permanent and remains, whereas that which is signified by the other, "non-skilled," is impermanent and does not remain. It is also apparent that the reality, the habit acquired, begins to be and is present only in the term *to which*. (That the skill is gradually perfected does not affect the case.) So with these points in front of us, we may now extend our considerations to include the coming to be of substances.

In all natural coming to be, something new begins to exist; for that is the meaning of "coming to be" and "becoming." Furthermore, that which comes to be comes to be from an antecedent-subject that remains throughout the becoming. But in order for something new to come to be from a subject, that which the subject acquires, and the subject itself, must be really (not just verbally) different; for a subject that is common to several things cannot account for their differences. In short, the notion of coming to be from a subject implies at least two principles: the term and the subject, the term being received by the subject. Aristotle does not explicitly mention this point in his own text, apparently because it is obvious; but we do so here for the sake of completeness.

The next point to be made is that the antecedent, although one in number, is formally two. But to see what this means we must begin with a difficulty.

As we saw, when the antecedent in a coming to be is signified simply, it can be signified either affirmatively or negatively. And from this double naming the difficulty arises, for it might be that only the names are multiple while the reality they signify is one; we do frequently call one thing by more than one name. Furthermore, the subject (*man* in Aristotle's example) is not the same reality as the term (*skilled* in the example), so we may say that the man is one of the realities in the category non-skilled. Thus it would seem that "subject" and "opposite" are two verbal signs for the same reality. If so, then there are only two principles of coming to be, not three as the names would suggest.

Aristotle, however, declares that this is not so, on the grounds that the subject and opposite are formally distinct in reality; their difference is not just verbal. So because two formalities can be distinguished in the antecedent, there are two different principles in it. And though we treated formal distinction in an earlier chapter, we shall repeat it here for the sake of making Aristotle's argument clear.

To say that the *significata* of two names are formally distinct is to say that they must be defined differently. If Socrates is a physician and builds a house, then we may say that *the physician builds a house*. Yet Socrates does not build the house insofar as he is a physician but insofar as he is a builder or carpenter. And though the art of medicine and the art of carpentry exist in the same subject, Socrates, they are different arts. On that account these two realities must be defined differently; their definitions cannot be arbitrary. And this is what it means to say that two *significata* are formally distinct.

Given what we have just said, we can see that the subject and the opposite must be formally distinct, they must be defined differently, because the subject remains throughout the becoming whereas the opposite does not. *Man* is still present when the *skilled man* comes to be, but *non-skilled* is not. Thus since *man* occurs when *non-skilled* is absent, the two are formally distinct. To put the matter another way, if *man* can be verified of the term *to which* at a time when *unskilled* cannot, then subject and opposite must be distinct. And what is true of the example is true of all coming to be.

It is necessary to note, however, that "opposites" are of more than one kind. In the present context the word signifies an incompatibility between two realities that are signified by terms which cannot be said of the same subject at the same time. The first kind of opposition is that which is represented by an affirmative term and its negation, as for example, *man* and *non-man*, *sighted* and *non-sighted*, *skilled* and *non-skilled*. The negative term of each pair simply removes that which is signified by the affirmative term, and therefore it can be predicated of anything that is different from that which is signified by the affirmative term. A rock is non-man, non-sighted, non-skilled; so is the number two. Opposition of this sort we shall call, following Aristotle, "contradictory opposition."

A second kind is called "privative opposition." Here one term signifies something affirmative or positive while the other signifies its absence, and to that extent privative is like contradictory opposition. A privative term, however, can be predicated only of the same kind of subject as the affirmative term that is paired with it. A privative name signifies a negation or absence in a determinate subject, for example, *blind* and *unskilled*. *Blind* can be said properly only of those animals which are endowed by nature with a power of sight, and *unskilled* can be said only of men. We may not say that stones are blind or that trees are unskilled, although we may say that stones are non-sighted and trees are non-skilled. In general, the negative term in privative opposition can be said only of those things that are ordinarily endowed with that which the affirmative term signifies, and it is to be said at a time when the latter is appropriately possessed. We do not consider newly born puppies to be blind, for they are not mature enough to see.

There is another kind of opposition in which the terms are opposed as extremes within a category of positive realities. For instance, "to succeed" and "to fail" divide a common category as extremes, for both success and failure are kinds of activity; one cannot fail if he does not try. "Kind" and "cruel" are opposites of this sort too, since a cruel act is not the same as no act. Such opposites, because both are within the same genus of reality, are related as the perfect to the imperfect; that is, one always lacks something of that which the other possesses. On that account the specific differences which define each are related as affirmative and negative. One difference will remove what the other posits; hence, one opposite will explicitly deny a part of what is contained in the notion of the other. Hard and soft are examples of this sort of opposition, for a soft body differs from a hard one in offering minimal resistance to a penetrating agent; a soft body does not lack all resistance. Finally, we must add that opposition of this sort is called "contrary opposition."

The last kind of opposition (correlative) involves pairs of terms in which one refers to the other in its understanding or definition; for instance, "teacher" implies "student" and "father" implies "child." Similarly, "whole" implies "part" and "ruler" the "ruled." Pairs of terms like this are not said of the same thing at the same time or in the same respect and for that reason are included under the notion of opposition. It is important to note, however, that neither term is negative, neither implies the absence of the other reality but instead requires its simultaneous existence.

To conclude our discussion of the distinction between subject and opposite, we may note that the opposite that is said of the term *from which* in a coming to be, will be either a privative opposite or a contrary opposite, for both are said of a limited subject, a subject that has a capacity to become what is produced. (Wherever there are contraries, there is privation, because one extreme lacks something of the other.) For instance, the unskilled becomes skilled, and the hard becomes soft. Thus because that which comes to be requires either a subject of which a contrary or a privative is said, the antecedent cannot be any reality whatsoever that is not the term. The skilled cannot come to be from anything whatsoever of which it is true to say that it is not a skill, but only from the unskilled.

Because that which comes to be cannot come to be from any antecedent whatsoever, but only from certain antecedents, we see that potentiality is not equivalent to non-existence. Gilbert Ryle would have us believe that there is no "third realm"[2] and that we must admit existence and non-existence but nothing that is neither of these in the full sense of each term. Yet that is precisely what a potentiality qua potentiality is; neither an actual existence nor a pure non-being. Plainly wood can become a wall stud but gelatin cannot, and so the potentiality we assign to the thing is not a fiction, a nothingness. In Ryle's view, to say that something is "able to be dissolved" is to say the equivalent of a conditional proposition: if sugar, for example, is placed in water under appropriate conditions, then it will dissolve. But this only pushes the problem back a step, for we still must ask why it is that we can formulate the conditional proposition about sugar and not about glass marbles. Thus we must admit that potentiality is a real property or characteristic of something that actually exists insofar as the latter can be something that it is not yet.

To summarize, then, we may say that coming to be requires three distinct principles: subject, term, and privation. Stated in the words we employed in the earlier chapters, coming to be requires a material, a structure, and a privation of the structure that is acquired.

B. The principles: two are per se and one is per accidens

We can see that the principles distinguished in the previous section are not alike, for two are per se and one is per accidens or incidental. To say that a principle is per se is to say that it is related to that of which it is the principle by reason of what it, the principle, is in itself. For instance, medicine is the per se cause of healing by reason of what it, the art of medicine, is in its own nature, whereas if the physician is also a carpenter, then carpentry is not of its nature related to curing the ill; yet because it is in the same person who is the physician, we may say that it is an incidental cause. Carpentry is, however, contingently related to curing the ill, for the physician does not have to possess it.

In order to show that the term and the subject are per se principles Aristotle argued as follows: anything from which a thing comes to be and exists is a per se principle; but the subject and term (material and structure) are that from which things come to be and exist; therefore they are per se principles. So the burden of his argument is that those elements which enter into the constitution of a thing as a consequence of a productive process are per se principles; and we recognize that as true. That privation, however, is not a per se principle is evident from its not entering into the constitution of the thing which comes to be. That from which something comes to be per se as an antecedent is the material, the potentiality, which means that privation is related to it as carpentry is to medicine in one who causes health; thus privation is a per accidens principle. But though it is a principle only incidentally, privation is unlike carpentry in the example above because it is a necessary principle, despite its incidental character. Privation is a necessary principle because in order for something to come to be it must first not exist. Moreover, privation is a principle only of becoming and not of the existence of the final product; for if it were a principle of existence, things would be inherently contradictions. Thus things do not come to be per se from non-being but from a potentiality.

The distinction made in the paragraph above allows us to understand the error inherent in Marxism. Dialectical materialism insists that opposites must exist together, and that all motion, development, and evolution are inherently contradictions. That there is a superficial appearance of cogency in this position is evident, for in order for a thing to come to be it must first of all not exist; it must come to be from that which is not the final product but can be the final product. If, now, we assume that the distinction between the subject or material on one hand and the privation on the other is not made, then things are contradictions. For if the privation is identified with the subject or material (a confusion of which Aristotle accuses Plato), then since the material and structure are correlative opposites they must exist together as the constituting elements of substances. Furthermore, since the privation has been identified with the material, it follows that that which is essentially non-being or absence is inherent within the constitution of the thing; and a thing would then contain its term and the (negative) opposite and so be a contradiction. That appears to be the confusion of which dialectical materialism is guilty.

With this we have finished. We could have made more extensive comments on the argument presented in the paragraphs above, but that would seem to be counterproductive, at least in these pages. More extensive elaborations ought to await another occasion.

Notes to Appendix

[1]Aristotle, *Physica*, Bk. I, cc. 7-9.

[2]*The Concept of Mind* (New York: Barnes & Noble, 1949). See pp. 88-89, and especially p. 119.

BIBLIOGRAPHY

The following is a bibliography of authors quoted in the essay.

BIBLIOGRAPHY

Aristotle. *The Works of Aristotle*. Ed. W.D. Ross. Oxford: At the Clarendon Press, 1912.

Barrow, Gordon M. *Physical Chemistry*. New York: McGraw-Hill Book Company, Inc., 1961.

Bierman, A. K. and James Gould, eds. "How the New Generation Got that Way." *Philosophy for a New Generation*. New York: The Macmillan Company, 1970.

Blanshard, Brand. "The Nature of Thought." *Metaphysics*. Eds. Julius R. Weinberg and Keith E. Yandell. New York: Holt, Rinehart and Winston, Inc., 1971.

Borst, Clive Vernon, ed. *Mind-Brain Identity Theory*. New York: St. Martin's Press, 1970.

Cantore, Enrico. *Atomic Order*. Cambridge, Massachusetts: The MIT Press, 1969.

Cornman, James W. *Materialism and Sensationalism*. New Haven and London: Yale University Press, 1971.

Davenport, Richard. *An Outline of Animal Development*. Reading, Massachusetts: Addison-Wesley Publishing Company, 1979.

Descartes, René. "Treatise on Man." *Descartes Selections*. Ed.
Ralph M. Eaton. New York: Charles Scribner's Sons.

Dicke, Robert. *Gravitation and the Universe*. Philadelphia:
American Philosophical Society, 1970.

Dodson, Edward O. *Evolution: Process and Product*. New York:
Rheinhold Publishing Company, 1960.

Eddington, Sir Arthur A. *New Pathways in Science*. Cambridge:
At the University Press, 1947.

Einstein, Albert and Leopold Infeld. *The Evolution of Physics*.
New York: Simon and Schuster, 1954.

Feigl, Herbert. "Mind-Body, not a Pseudo-Problem." *Mind-Brain
Identity Theory*. Ed. Clive Vernon Borst. New York: St.
Martin's Press, 1970.

Granit, Ragnar. *The Purposive Brain*. Cambridge, Massachusetts:
The MIT Press, 1977.

Haemmerling, J. "The Role of the Nucleus in Differentiation
Especially in Acetabularia." Reprinted in *Molecular and
Cellular Aspects of Development*. Ed. Eugene Bell. New York:
Harper & Row, Publishers, 1967.

Ham, Arthur W. and Daniel H. Cormads. *Histology*. Philadelphia
and Toronto: J. B. Lippencott Company, 1979.

Heisenbeurg, Werner. *Physics and Philosophy*. New York: Harper
and Brothers, 1958.

Herschel, Sir William. "On Nebulous Stars." *Classics of Modern
Science*. Ed. William S. Knickerbocker. Boston: Beacon Press,
1962.

Hobbes, Thomas. *Leviathan*. The Crowell-Collier Publishing
Company, 1962.

Hume, David. *A Treatise of Human Nature*. Ed. Selby-Biggs. Oxford: The Clarendon Press, 1975.

Knutson, Eric I. "The Hearing of the Barn Owl." *Scientific American*, Dec. 1981.

Kremyanskiy, V. I. "Certain Peculiarities of Organisms as a 'System' from the Point of View of Physics, Cybernetics and Biology." Trans. Anatol Rapoport in *General Systems*. Reprinted in *Modern Systems Research for the Behavioral Scientist*. Ed. Walter Buckley. Chicago: Adaline Publishing Co., 1968.

Lazerowitz, Morris. "Substratum." *Philosophical Analysis*. Ed. Max Black. Englewood Cliffs, N. J.: Prentice-Hall, Inc., 1963.

Leibniz, Gottfried Wilhelm. *Leibniz*. Trans. George A. Montgomery. La Salle, Illinois: The Open Court Publishing Co., 1962.

Levin, Michael. *Metaphysics and the Mind-Body Problem*. Oxford: The Clarendon Press, 1979.

Lewis, Gilbert Newton and Merle Randall. *Thermodynamics*. 2nd ed. New York: McGraw-Hill Book Company, Inc., 1961.

Lwoff, André. *Biological Order*. Cambridge, Massachusetts: The MIT Press, 1968.

Materials. A Scientific American Book. San Francisco: W. J. Freeman and Company, 1967.

Monod, Jacques. *Chance and Necessity*. Trans. Austryn Wainhouse. New York: Vintage Books, 1972.

Nagel, Ernest. *The Structure of Science*. New York: Harcourt, Brace & World, Inc., 1961.

Nebergall, William, Frederic C. Schmidt, and Henry F. Haltzslaw,

Jr. *College Chemistry*. Lexington, Massachusetts: D. C. Heath and Company, 1976.

Oparin, A. I. *The Origin of Life on the Earth*. Trans. Ann Synge. New York: Academic Press, Inc., 1957.

Piaget, Jean. *The Child's Conception of the World*. Trans. Joan and Andrew Tomlinson. Totowa, New Jersey: Littlefield, Adams & Co., 1965.

Polyani, Michael. "Life's Irreducible Structure." *Science*. 160 (21 June 1968), 1308-12.

Price, H. H. "Appearing and Appearances." *American Philosophical Quarterly*. Vol. I, No.1, Jan. 1964.

Quinton, Anthony. *The Nature of Things*. London: Routledge & Kegan Paul, 1972.

Rensch, Bernard. "Polynomistic Determination of Biological Process." *Studies in the Philosophy of Biology*. Eds. Francisco José Ayola and Theodosius Dobzhansky. Berkeley and Los Angeles: University of California Press, 1974.

_____. "Evolution of Matter and Consciousness and its Relation to Pansychistic Idealism." *Essays in Evolution and Genetics in Honor of Theodosious Dobzhansky*. New York: Appleton-Century Crofts, 1970.

Russell, E. S. *The Behavior of Animals*. London: Edward Arnold & Co., 1934.

_____. *The Directiveness of Organic Activities*. Cambridge: At the University Press, 1944.

Seifriz, William. "A Materialistic Interpretation of Life." *Philosophy of Science*. Vol. 6 (1939).

Shortley, George and Dudley Williams. *Physics*. New York: Prentice-Hall, Inc., 1950.

Simpson, George Gaylord, Colin S. Pittendrigh, and Lewis Tiffany.
    Life. New York: Harcourt, Brace and Company, Inc., 1957.

Sinnott, Edmund W. *The Biology of Spirit*. London: Victor
    Gollancz, Ltd., 1956.

Stevens, Charles S. "The Neuron." *Scientific American*.
    September 1979.

Storer, John H. *The Web of Life*. New York: The New American
    Library, Inc., 1956.

Sullivan, Thomas D. "The Status of Meaning: Between Thoughts
    and Things." *The New Scholasticism*, 50 (Winter 1976).

Swanson, Carl P. *The Cell*. Englewood Cliffs, New Jersey:
    Prentice-Hall, Inc., 1960.

Vander, Arthur J., James H. Sherman, and Dorothy S Luciano.
    Human Physiology. New York: McGraw-Hill, Inc., 1970.

Von Bertalanffy, Ludwig. *Problems of Life*. New York: John Wiley
    and Sons, Inc., 1952.

_____. *Modern Theories of Development*. New
    York: Harper & Brothers, 1962.

_____. *General Systems Theory*. New York:
    George Braziller, 1968.

Von Buddenbrock, Wolfgang. *The Senses*. Ann Arbor, Michigan:
    The University of Michigan Press, 1958.

INDEX

Wisdom from St. Augustine
Vernon J. Bourke

Fourteen very readable articles gathered from many periodicals.

About Beauty:
A Thomistic Interpretation
Armand A. Maurer, C.S.B.

An Interpretation of Existence
Joseph Owens, C.Ss.R.

An Elementary Christian Metaphysics
Joseph Owens, C.Ss.R.

A Catalogue of Thomists, 1270-1900
Leonard A. Kennedy, C.S.B.

The names and works of over 2000 writers with a Thomist
reputation, arranged by century, country, and (where applicable)
religious community.

Known from the Things that Are:
Fundamental Theory of the Moral Life
Martin D. O'Keefe, S.J.

A theoretical and applied treatment of ethics. The
argumentation throughout is philosophical, and no conclusions
contradict the teaching of the Church's Magisterium.